I WAS ALSO THERE

Laima Leyton

Embodied memories of this name, I also carry
From invaded lands and religion as a weapon
Where then my spirituality gets lost.

You try to find it
To heal it
To express it
To contain it
To embody it
To manifest it
To echo and reverberate
In memory, through image, sound, energy
Non-linear time and space.

We were all meant to be there,
And to be where we were
Where we are
We were there
We are here
Non-linear time and space.

We try to witness,
To be compassionate
To hold
To care
To heal.

The memory of a body that heals
Heals while in pain
Heals to transcend
The mother
The grandmother
You and
The other.

If loss were a currency:
on Kamila Kuc's *I Was There*

First published 2025
by Delere Press

ISBN 978-981-94-2877-9

Cover and Typesetting   Sarah and Schooling
Typefaces   Public Sans, Bembo

If loss were a currency:
on Kamila Kuc's *I Was There*

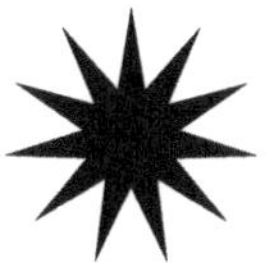

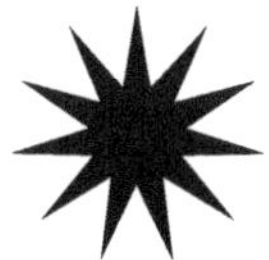

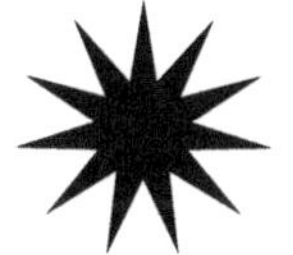

Laima Leyton
Dara Waldron
Ecka Mordecai
Jeremy Fernando
Kamila Kuc

CONTENTS

IT WAS TIME, IT IS TIME.

Dara Waldron

Embracing we stand by the window, and people look
up from
the street
It is time that they knew!
It is time that the stone grew accustomed to
blooming,
that unrest formed a heart.
It is time it was time.

It is time.

~ Paul Celan, *Corona*.

I landed in Melbourne a few days before Kamila's email
arrived in my inbox. It was an invite to write a text about
her new film *I Was There* for a book published to coincide
with the film's release. A personal film about her grandmother
Helena's near death during the German invasion of Poland.
A film about witnessing evil. Would I write something in
response to the film as part of the text? Not an academic text,
the email stresses, nor a book of poetry. What kind of text? I
wonder. Maybe it's not quite a book, in the conventional sense,
but a text-like prod to think. I start to think of what to write.
I think of the controversy around Jonas Mekas in the years
before his death. Accused by the Jewish American historian
Michael Casper of bending the truth about his experiences in
Lithuania prior to becoming a displaced person in Germany,
the question that burned in response goes like this: 'was he
there?' The question is a reference to the killings in the forests
of Biržai, near the village that gave us Jonas Mekas. At times
in his life, once when speaking to graduates in Philadelphia,
Mekas references the forest killings, like he was there, faced

with the incomprehensible horror. The Mekas discourse that percolates in the aftermath of the accusations, with filmmakers, historians, archivists, and fans all dipping in, coalesces around issues of memory, and perhaps, even *postmemory*, as Marianne Hirsch calls it. 'I was there' is a de facto truth for Casper. You are or you are not *there*. There is no middle ground in this, no nuance in thinking between the physical bearing of weight in a particular place and the possibility of being somewhere as a metaphysical realisation of post memory. What if you were not there? And yet somehow there in spirit, caught in the storm of reverberations that remain in awkward stares, silence, strange redux of imaginings and dreams.

Kamila understands this, I think, more than most. It is the reason why her film, at times in the form of a double and even three-screen installation, begins with a shot of the autobiographical filmmaker, walking naked from a beach cave into the light. The obvious reference point here is Plato's cave, the philosophical allegory that begets an understanding of form and essence, the transient and Ideal. The grainy, glitchy analogue that makes it difficult to profile the artist's movement from the cave is an echo of the Platonic difficulty of seeing beyond the walls of the cave itself. Difficult, yes. But not impossible. As Kamila's nude profile appears through the haze, the suggestion is again Platonic – the essence of things can now be seen. Time is inoperative: there is only Helena's crackly voice we hear and so many things to serve as reminders of the implicit horror of *that day*, as time itself stands still. It is the day Helena's beloved were killed as partisans in a war they did not start or want.

If loss was a currency, you'd be rich, but loss is a country, and you're poor

Jonas kept on making films about his life, endlessly circling around the void. Loss was a country that he kept returning to from the US. The real question, however, is whether he left the cave? Maybe, Jonas had been there, in the forests of Biržai, in his head, his bones, his memory. The collapse of one person's memory into another, sometimes called postmemory, sometimes intergenerational trauma, is premised on a feeling of dislocation: of being there but not feeling as if one is participating in the now as it pertains to that illusive construct: presence. 'I was there' is a far more complicated statement than a simple utterance implies. The 'I', in some instances, is fragmented, multiple, displaced into a distant future the artist seeks to occupy.

But the past keeps pulling her back. Poland, her grandmother spared by a strange ruling on partisanship, her uncles, the family, her kin, murdered in cold blood. After the most onerous details of her grandmother's story are told, a life caught up in somebody else's war, the cave and Kamila's exit from it, returns. The cliffs seem easier to see in the background, as the naked figure appears on a beach splintered in coloured pixels of film. Kamila states 'my best version of Polish is silence,' a statement that in equal levels of complexity and simplicity invokes the ghost of Chantal Akerman. Akerman, a child of a Holocaust survivor, is drawn, throughout her difficult life to traces of *time* that percolate in the present as spectres: in queues for food in Eastern Europe, the train stations across the land. New York, where Jonas found reprieve. She tried, with each film she made, to leave the cave. But she was pulled back until finally in defeat.

The double collapses into one screen – suggesting some temporary reprieve – as Kamila's profile collapses into the spectre of her grandmother. Dressed in tight fitting black clothing, appearing modern and in control, her physical movements are reminiscent of the patterns of movements children make when isolated from parents, neurotically hitting themselves to stay stimulated: like the children of Romanian orphanages left idly alone. Kamila's gestures are inward in this way, physical attempts to release trauma nestled in the body, idle and unspoken. When thinking of the orphans who invoke these rhythmic gestures to make up for love, I also think of Marina Abramovich, who, if I am not mistaken, wore similar tight-fitting clothing for the rhythmic, ritualistic performances choreographed to physically expel the residue of trauma.

At certain points in *I Was There,* the two screens that purposefully play off against each other dissolve into one. The dissolution becomes a single screened impression of Kamila's choreographed movement as a performing artist. Echoing the disturbed movement of a child forced to self-soothe, the gestures are an attempt to expel the demonic known as trauma. This is Helena Kuc's story as it is passed down in time to her granddaughter. A granddaughter who loved her, dearly. Love is not the One but as Alain Badiou says, the Two that gives life to the One. A physical movement that embodies and therefore recognises her grandmother as part of the self. A poem that is spoken against physical movements, unholy gestures into memory's abyss:

Bowing to the rich landowner and his wife,
Bowing to the priest,
Kneeling in church,
Kneeling while digging potatoes,
Bending low carrying buckets of water,
Bending low boiling potatoes for the pig's dinner,
Bending low churning butter,
Bending low with children on your back,
Bending low with children in your belly.

There is a powerful affect to this – brought on by an eerie compulsion to explain – as the harrowing personal sequence. The voice over (performed by Ecka Mordercai, also the film's sound artist) impersonates Kamila's lines against salient images of repetitious physical exertion: like ritualistic drumming.

However incongruous the movements in fact are, whether
as dance or repetitious cycles of trauma, they nonetheless
chime in a poetic manner with the embodied recognition
of an elder's pain: the grandmother whose story stirs like an
affliction within the blood when fully recognised as such. This
isn't just a retelling of familial trauma. It is a sequence of film
that illustrates the difficulty retelling a narrative that has been
passed down through the family. This is a curse percolating over
time. 'Postmemory,' as Hirsch describes it (in a study of creative
work evolving from the inheritance of trauma, both personally
delivered but also shaped by the greater public narratives
that allude to the trauma the child has not lived through), is
defined by an unwanted inheritance: the feeling of not being
worthy: *not* having lived through. Is it any wonder that the
film that springs to mind when watching *I Was There* is Claude
Lanzmann's *Shoah*? The field, the river behind where men are
shot, the sharing of experience in testimony from Poland, are all
echoes of the Holocaust spreading itself across Eastern Europe,
filtered through re-enactments of evil on *film*.

'Postmemory is a powerful tool and a very particular type of
memory,' Hirsch writes 'precisely because its connection to
its object or source is mediated not through recollection but
through an imaginative investment and creation.' *I Was There*
is characterised by depictions of an artist *becoming* the 'source'
itself – in perceived solidarity, imaginative reinvestment,
and creation. Kamila wears her grandmother's shirt; speaks
of wanting to live in her house. She desires, evidently, to
embody her. To give to numbness the visceral redeem. To
go past pain. But frustration is not being able to, reduced to
making gestures that look and feel like wringing pain from
a body – setting it free. 'Postmemory,' Hirsch writes of this
complex, 'characterizes the experience of those who grow up
dominated by narratives that preceded their birth, whose own
belated stories are evacuated by the stories of the previous

generation shaped by traumatic events that can neither be understood nor recreated.' *Neither understood nor recreated.*

The postmemory condition stirs in recurring attempts to narrativize what exceeds narrative convention, to squash memory of an event as it percolates in the mind of the offspring, bastardised and undone by a culture that recycles stories of trauma to feed the culture industry. No poetry after Auschwitz, but bucket loads of recycled thrash. *Instead, I went back to the sea* Kamila retorts, giving context to the opening scene documenting a nude granddaughter walking on a beach. The medical advice given to her abused grandmother is to have some time at the sea, to which Kamila's response more than half a century later, is still one of anger. How to dispel the anger? How to push it down so that it manifests in creative outputs about Eastern Europe that include extensive reference to the sea: *Batum, What We Shared* (Kuc's previous films), etc? Sublimated attempts to get at the THING that nestles in the body and resists being encompassed into narrative form.

How to give it up? Give it some air to breathe and therefore banish it from an all-encompassing now. Make a film in which two screens divide the visual plane. But that unite in moments and become a third screen. Devise it as an installation. Make a book about it that gives it a memorial presence. Maybe you can invite some friend scholars to write a response, heartfelt and not too academic, about the emotional impact of this powerful piece, soaked into the blood of several generations of Kucs.

After sending out the invite, maybe one of the invitees will sit in ACMI in Melbourne on the 16 December 2024, watching two films by the Karrabing Film Collective, *A Day in the Life* and *The Family and the Zombie.* After the screening is a Q & A with members of the indigenous Aboriginal family that make up the collective, of which three generations are present for the discussion. The invitee, also known as me, will listen to the collective speak of sustained attacks on their way of life over decades, the sacred nature of their land. And then an elder, speaking about some of the younger generation, mentions 'intergenerational trauma' like the concept circulates widely, in the vernacular, everywhere. But this is not the case. The term is relatively new. The Karrabing Collective want to stay close to the land, but others want to stay close to the sea. The signifiers 'land' and 'sea' are marked by intergenerational trauma, the artist's job is to wrench then free from one context, to invest the signifier with new meaning: to make images interact, dance like words in a poem after Auschwitz. And then we can declare: *it is time*.

NOTES FROM A FIELD

Ecka Mordecai

The Field

The field is a place of violence articulated by crickets.

The indifference of their stridulation meets Helena's story which is ardently factual, concise. If Kamila's "version of Polish is silence," her grandmother's version of silence is a narrative devoid of affect: she doesn't tell us how she feels, she doesn't tell us what happened to her, only *what happened*.

The skeletal manner of her speaking reminds me of a dried seed: genetically complete yet lacking life, we can't witness its unfolding, flowering, its fleshing out. Instead, we follow the trails of her voice broken by poor quality audio.

Kamila embodies: filling the gaps, germinating the seed and becoming flesh, the sun-kissed wheat below dazzling skies. She's right here, medium and conduit. Her gaze cascades upon us and tells us that she was there, too.

The crickets. I'll explain how they became The Field's *keynote*[1]...

---

[1] In soundscape studies, keynote sounds are those which are heard by a particular society continuously or frequently enough to form a backdrop against which other sounds are perceived.

Michel Chion, *Sound: An Acoulogical Treatise*, translated by James. A. Steintrager. Durham: Duke University Press, 2016, 9.

Late summer, my feelings were hurting and I wanted to be alone in nature, unhinged. I'd spent all week in the studio failing to compose something expressive of *anxiety-in-a-state-of-dissociation*, which I needed to confer the dichotomy of Kamila's anxiety and Helena's apparent dissociation.

Before work on Friday I packed a bag containing a tent, sleeping bag, 500g pasta, 50ml olive oil, salt and pine nuts, two bottles of soju, a portable stove, soap, two microphones and an audio recorder.

I planned to arrive at Cuckmere Haven before sunset.

The Haven is a small cove at the foot of the Seven Sisters white chalk cliffs, the tallest being a notable suicide spot. I was in the final throes of grieving the death of my friend Lou, who loved it here, and filled with volatile emotion I was playing 'field recordist' in a tragic attempt to get as close as geographically possible to the nerve center of British suicide. I wanted to understand how people do it.

The sun was a giant red orb lilting into a gentle landscape and up on the cliffs I saw a tent being battered by the wind. I wasn't alone. Had I expected to be?

Snaking past a group of horses and a ground-nesting site for seabirds, I heard grasshoppers. The way to distinguish a grasshopper from a cricket, sonically, is time: grasshoppers chirp only during the day, crickets chirp both day and night.

I pitched my tent in a recess slightly back from the beach. The ground was soft and mossy and the waves crashed onto nearby beach-pebbles, amplified by reverberation from the cliff-face. During the war, concave listening points were installed along this stretch of coastline to allow frontline soldiers to hear the enemy approaching by foot. Someone told me the beaches around here used to be sandy, that the military had brought pebbles to make it difficult for the French to sneak up on us. Judging by the surrounding geology I'd have guessed the pebbles were natural, and I sensed this person didn't like the French. Nonetheless, it's a good sonic anecdote, real or imagined.

I made my bed for the night and started cooking pasta when I saw a figure descending the last of the Sisters. I went inside the tent and after a few minutes heard footsteps approach in the twilight. Wild camping in England is illegal, so I decided to stick my head out the tent and smile nicely, hoping this wasn't a National Trust warden.

"Oh, thank god you're a woman!"

Gosia had come down from the cliff because it was too windy and she was afraid of camping alone. Like Kamila she grew up in Poland and she's similarly blonde-haired and beautiful and has the endearing quality of being both very strong and very sensitive. I liked her a lot and we walked the cliffs and camped together for three days, aside from the moments I went off alone to record.

I told her about Kamila and the film and made her cry. She said it was expressive of a nationally-shared grief. I feel it too, in my Jewishness. I'm also there.

We all are.

On the Sisters we talked about death and suicide, and her fears that once we die that's it: nothing. I stopped and reflected upon my own belief in reincarnation and the afterlife. Where did I inherit that from? My mother? Her mother? Her mother's mother? Is it a belief I carried over from a past life?

On the final day, we arose amidst the gorse bushes, completely saturated by sun and a shrill insectile continuum. A rescue helicopter came and went and I stood atop the highest cliff, tried to imagine jumping.

I thought of Lou and watched thousands of white butterflies silently grace the horizon. I cried, listening to the sea; and trying to block out the crickets, whose endless chant offered no solace. They were getting on my nerves, not only because they wouldn't shut up but because of their indifference to human pain. They were there when Helena's father and the other village men were taken to the field and shot dead. Why did they sing? They witnessed Helena being raped by the farmer, still a child working the land in bare feet. Why were they singing? And they're here, now; their shrill little hearts cascading across the landscape and out to sea, upon a cliff where many come to die, the last sound they'll ever hear.

The Sea

The sea is a site of healing where solar winds swept us onto the endless sands. I sat perfectly still, pointing a microphone at Kamila's feet as she pressed bare skin into hundreds of razor clam shells abandoned by the birds. They cracked against the whispering breeze, out to the horizon marked by maritime industry and a cloudless sky.

I held a smooth, warm, hollow eggshell against the wind aeolian and thought about women.

Time

At one minute past midnight in the perfectly vertical posture of my childhood I listened to my grandmother's chiming clock decay into night, a soft ticking, the gentle thin light of a full moon falling through the open window.

I'd left my mother sleeping in a nearby room, a room with a very high ceiling and large walnut wardrobes and two single beds weighed down by thick woollen blankets smelling faintly damp. A fireplace, dark and unlit. Heavy velvet curtains blocking all natural light, the digital alarm clock my only tool for navigation.

Upstairs, my grandmother, Marjorie, was sleeping next to her fluffy white cat whose eyes were a glazed milky blue due to blindness. She was inside the blankets, coiled in a silent and perfect circle.

This is the place I learned to be a daughter: through observing my mother as one. Seeing her in proximity to my grandmother helped me understand her anxieties and how she became so needy. Like Helena, my grandmother was stoic, and this brought out the victim in my mother and consequently the stoic in me. Does matriarchal logic always follow this route? Do we strive to compensate the other? Is this how, as women, we navigate care?

When Marjorie died my mother inherited the grandmother clock that had stood tall in the corridor of that big old townhouse in Liverpool, beside the open window at midnight. Its chimes mimic the great bells of Westminster Abbey and its gentle ticking falls slightly off-beat. I recorded the clock and named the files 'grandmother time,' gifting them to Helena in the soundtrack.

Grandmother clock tells us to listen, that it's time to hear stories previously untold.

The Body

The cello is a body is a vessel a reproductive vessel a woman
a sexualised woman object not fetishised per se but certainly
adored and expected to do what it's told.

When I was learning to play the cello at school I was learning
to reproduce the works of dead men. Was I a medium? Is that
mediumship? Why did it feel so uncomfortable, my back arched
and my legs spread apart? Later in her career, the British cellist
Jaqueline Du Pré believed her cello was haunted. Haunted
by a heavy history of composers, of her own mediumship, or
something else? Our bodies are sounding media, but who and
what are we sounding?

Learning the cello is a game of perfectionist mimicry but once
I stopped taking lessons and went to art school I loved the
instrument for its presence and not its potential.

I loved the old wood, the way it smelled, the way I could pick
it up and pretend to waltz. I left it in the cold and pulled it into
bed with me, feeling the wood contract and creak slightly in
response to my body heat.

I held it between my thighs, breathing deep and playing one
single note for a whole hour. I got into free-improv and
developed a collection of extended techniques.

Tōru Takemitsu taught me about *sawari* which, when speaking of
instruments, refers to something placed intentionally to touch or
obstruct the string, producing a kind of micronoise. Rather than
listening for the sustain and decay, or attention is re-routed to the
material of the sound itself, the now, the thing itself.

When he died, Helena was freed from her husband and
the body he gave her. No longer bending low, she is light-

footed and upright, soundtracked by harmonic drones on cello. Harmonics resonate at a higher frequency than the fundamental, giving a sense of freedom and transcendence but I chose to record so close to the bow that you can hear the scraping of horsehair against metal. It's uncomfortably intimate and the *sawari* of the recording holds us within this discomfort, despite the worst of her story being over.

Why couldn't I give that to you, listener? Why couldn't I set Helena free? It's the same reason I couldn't sonically dramatise her early experiences, no matter how traumatic I perceived them to be, because I was there too, entangled in that messy subjectivity in which there is no release, or escape, or resolution, but there is an opportunity to feel and touch, to be present and honest and here.

Never contaminate fiction with a message.
On the contrary, I believe fiction is a search shared with the reader.

~ Luisa Valenzuela

The work of writing is always done in relation to something that no longer exists, which may be fixed for a moment in writing, like a trace, but which has vanished. I don't know how the present intervenes …

~ Georges Perec

Why can't we accept the fact that the right thing to do is live inside this very special tension which keeps suicide suspended?

~ Franz Kafka to Milena Jesenská, affectionately

TU ÉTAIS LÀ ? MOI AUSSI,
MOI NON PLUS ...

Jeremy Fernando

Letters, post-cards, missives, films ... who knows when they land, where they do if they do, if we even know whenever they do, if we take what has landed as something for us, as if it were for us ...

... and why we are so concerned with landings, with land, *terroir* — it could well be a question of territory, being territorial (« war for territory », scream Sepultura, in protest no less, *o seu grito, o nosso grito, talvez até inscrito em nós ... como escrita*[1]) — with grounds, being grounded ...

... why not flights, even those of fancy, lightness ...

... after all, it is cinema, *movements of blocks of time* involving *the writing of light*, it be cinema we are watching, seeing, hearing, feeling, attempting to bear witness to ...

Ah, feeling ... senses ... the sensual ...

... aisthesis

---

[1] your cry, our cry, perhaps even inscribed in us ...
  like writing

[I]

28

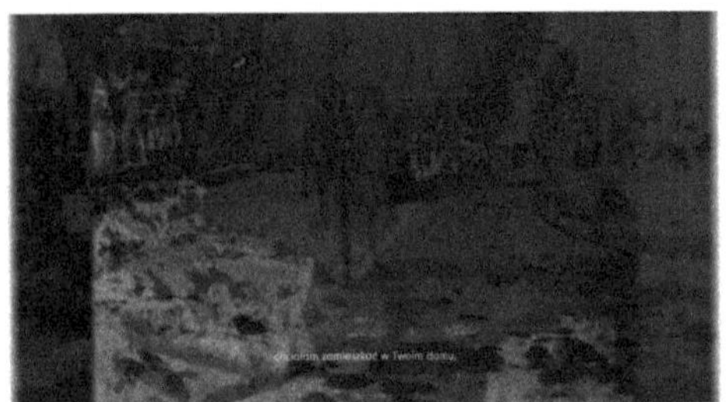

She walks, who is she?, let me know if you could, you know how to reach me, through the page; if only there were still pagers, but you can always still get in touch.

Ah to touch,
perchance to dream.

And speaking of dreams, I would like to think she were walking onto a beach. But really all I can see, and what is reading but attempting to see, to really see, not what we want to see but what is there, seeing also with your fingers, digits. So not just you touching the page, but also the page paging you.

Impagination.

She is walking into blue.

So perhaps all I can try to do is « place a delphinium, blue, upon your grave ».

*I have walked
behind the sky*

~ Derek Jarman

And maybe, just maybe, like the « I » in *Blue*, she has too,
but just *into*.

[II]

30

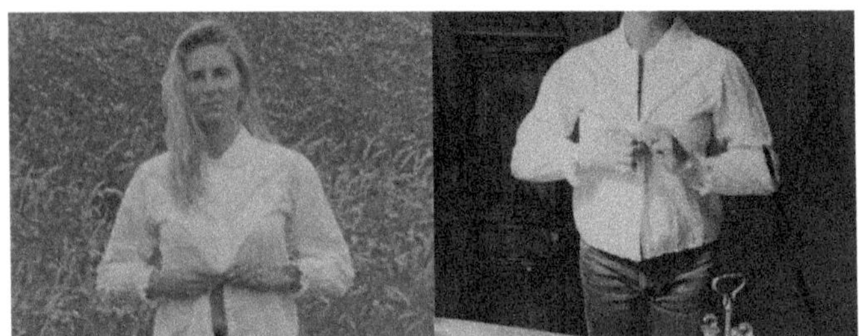

Buttons.

They hold together, yet ensure that even in coming-together the two halves stay slightly apart.

Giving just enough room to touch. Ah, tender buttons.

For, « it is space that is first needed for touch » (Jean-Luc Nancy).

To caress perhaps.

We cannot possess gentleness. We offer it hospitality. It is there, as discreet and necessary and vital as a heartbeat. Its carnal power goes from sensuousness to the lightest pressure of the hand; it is thought when it touches and touched when it is intelligence.

~ Anne Dufourmantelle

To touch, perchance to dream.

La chose
La toucher
Bousculer
La forme.

~ Pierre Alferi[2]

---

[2] *The thing*
Touch it
Jostle
The form.

~ Pierre Alferi

And, there is also no greater joy than in bringing dear friends together in words, in worlds, especially when they are no longer in our world.

Such is the beauty — and sadness — of memory.

A dash;
it links — but also ensures the two remain apart.

And be careful you don't, in your haste, excitement, frantic desire to be together, dash towards too quickly, less you be dashed ... apart.

[III]

33

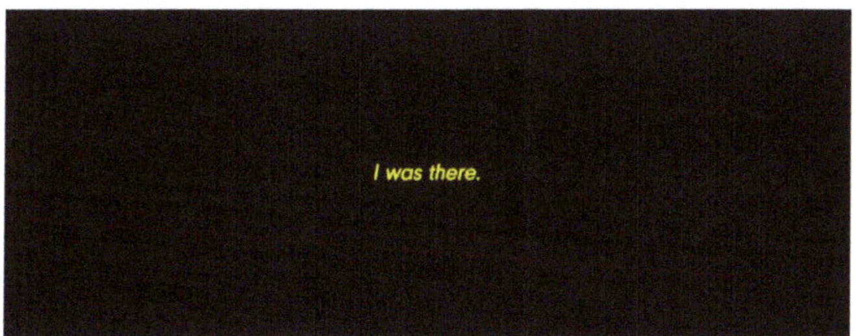

White on white translucent landscapes
Back on the rack
Bela Lugosi's dead
The bats have left the bell tower
The victims have been bled
Red velvet lines the black box
Bela Lugosi's dead

~ Bauhaus, *jf remix*

My best version of Polish is silence

I sometimes wonders if *silence speaks loudest* not only because it signals to an absence, or an inability to articulate despite wanting to, but that it reminds us that even in whatever is said, uttered, yelled, cried-out[3] there is always also an accompanying silence, a silence accompanying it.

---

[3]As Nietzsche★ continues to remind us, in every writing (*schreiben*) there is also a certain scream (*schreien*). And nothing is quite as terrifying as a silent scream.

For, as Kafka★★ never quite lets us forget, « the Sirens have a still more fatal weapon than their song, namely their silence. And though admittedly such a thing has never happened, still it is conceivable that someone might possibly have escaped from their singing; but from their silence certainly never ».

And that the frown on Odysseus' face — the very sign that signaled to his companions they could release him from the mast, the one that was supposed to mark the fact that he was no longer under the spell of the Siren's song — was due to the fact that all he heard was their « silence ».

Which might well mean that even though he escaped that one time, the song (and since he's never yet heard the song, quite possibly any song) is always also awaiting him. Or, even worse, that each time he sees water, the memory of the « silence », of the possibility of the song, haunts him.

Even if he might have tried to put it behind him, attempted to have forgotten.

For, as John Irving never lets us forget: « your memory is a monster, you forget — it doesn't. It simply files things away. It keeps things for you, or hides things from you — and summons them to your recall with a will of its own. You think you have a memory; but it has you! »

Where each song, every song, any song — or, even worse, any silence, every silence — is quite possibly their song.

Jeremy Fernando

All I ever wanted
All I ever needed
Is here in my arms
Words are very unnecessary
They can only do harm

~ Depeche Mode

Sshhhhhhh !

Awaiting the moment, their moment, to wash over him again.

★ Why does the poor man always lose his first name whenever we speak
of, write about, him? One might call it *rising to the heights of fame*, where
one is only known by a single name: Cher, Prince, Bono, Madonna.
But at the same time, an absolute reduction to whatever is associated
with said single-name: where there is only a singleness to you, and all
multiplicity has been stripped away.

So, with a *mea culpa* to Friedrich Wilhelm Nietzsche for the above.

★★ likewise to Franz Kafka.

And:

I say this to whoever wants to listen: when we believe we see the life and work
fusing in the figure of a writer, let us consider that their life is deliberately false
and has been invented solely to support the work, which truly is real.

~ Enrique Vila-Matas

[IV]

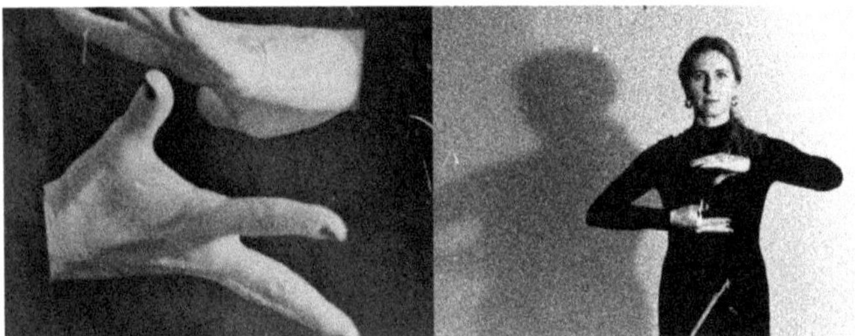

*Parataxis is a strange literary form, born at the beginning of
the Middle Ages. Old epic stories that had once been handed
down by tribal elders pass into the hands of storytellers.
Flashing back and sideways, holding back the outcome of
events, these tellers fracture old familiar and heroic tales into
contradictory, multiple perspectives. It becomes impossible to
move the story forward without returning to the past, and so
the past both predicates the future and withholds it.*

~ Chris Kraus

In your hands you hold — not so much the tale (that would be unfair
on you, and your hands, and the story) but — the *space* for the yarn to
begin to spin (itself).

After all, like with all things, but especially those which are fragile,
malleable, sensual, hold on too tightly and they slip, squirm, fly away
(*s'envoler*), sometimes like a thief (*une voleuse*) in the night[4] …

But give them enough room, shelter them, hide them away — just a
little away from the glare of the world — *se transformer en arbre*, provide
habour, be their veil (*soit leur voile*) and they might well turn into a sail
(*une voile*).[5]

*Bodies, for good or ill, are touching each other upon
this page, or more precisely, the page itself is a touching
(of my hand while it writes, and your hands while
they hold the book).*

~ Jean-Luc Nancy

---

[4] … and like with all nightly flights, quite possibly taking your heart
away. Even with words, especially with tales. As the great Australian
philosophers — Barry, Maurice, and Robin, Gibb — continue to teach
us, « it's only words, and words are all I have, to take your heart away ».

[5] *Fly me to the moon
And let me play among the stars*

~ Kaye Ballard

[V]

38

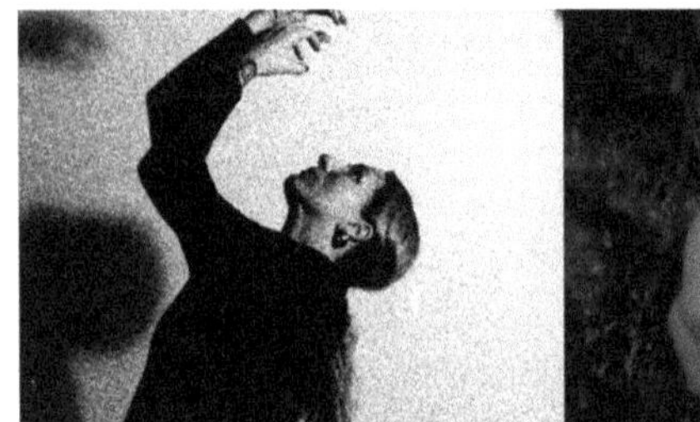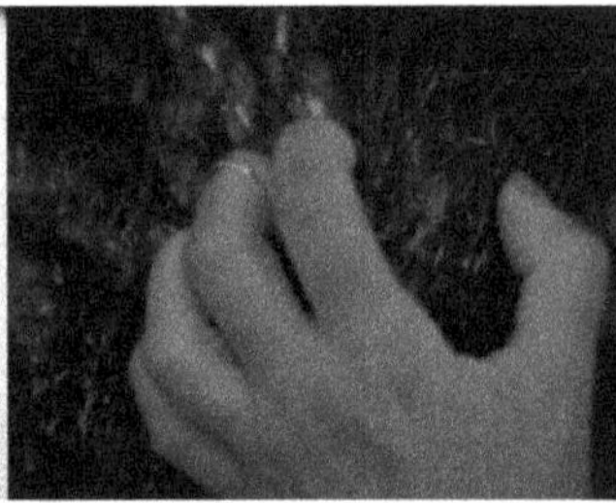

The only part of our bodies we can truly see be our hands.

One might even say they often call out to us, coming into our line of sight, even crossing it, often even directing it, pointing out where we should look. Occasionally one suspects they might well be whispering, see me, see me; so much so that even as we think we use them to gesture, to speak-with, it be actually our hands who are speaking … through us.

Suivant mes mains,

> *j'écris au rythme, cela fait loi en moi. C'est très sensuel. Les langues sont des anges à mémoire. Elles gardent et répètent le pas de Kleist ou celui de Büchner ou celui de Stendhal, le souffle, la course.*
>
> ~ Hélène Cixous[6]

But you are not merely looking, for you, you who so good with words, so with worlds, but above all with seeing, with opening yourself to see,[7] know they are also looking at you — digitally.

A touch see.

---

[6] Following my hands, « I write to the rhythm, it is the law in me. It is very sensual. Languages are angels with memories. They keep and repeat the step of Kleist or that of Büchner or that of Stendhal, the breath, the race » (Hélène Cixous).

[7] And if we open ourselves to the whispers of Marguerite Duras resounding here, we can also hold on to the possibility that *whenever there is seeing, there is also the sea.*

So maybe not so much a hear-say, but a hear-sea, here-see.

Et tes mains, elles aussi, écrivent leur propre rythme. Peut-être que tout ce que nous devons faire, c'est apprendre à les écouter.

Piano piano.

Moderato cantabile.[8]

---

[8] And your hands, they too, write their own rhythm. Maybe all we need to do is learn to listen to them.

Softly softly.

Moderately and singingly.

[VI]

41

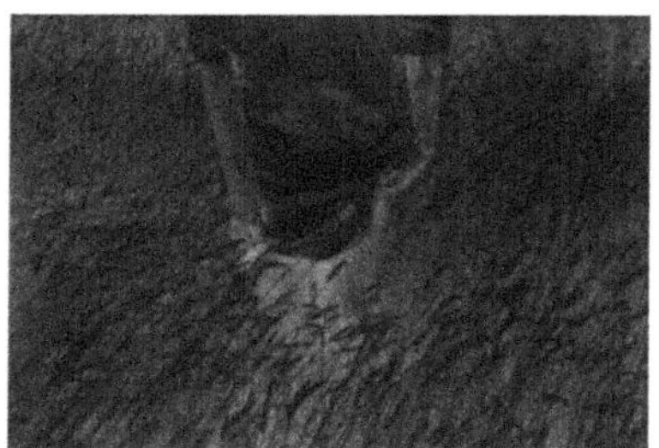

Plausible union,
man and tree.
Teach me to stand still.

~ Robert Kelly

[VII]

43

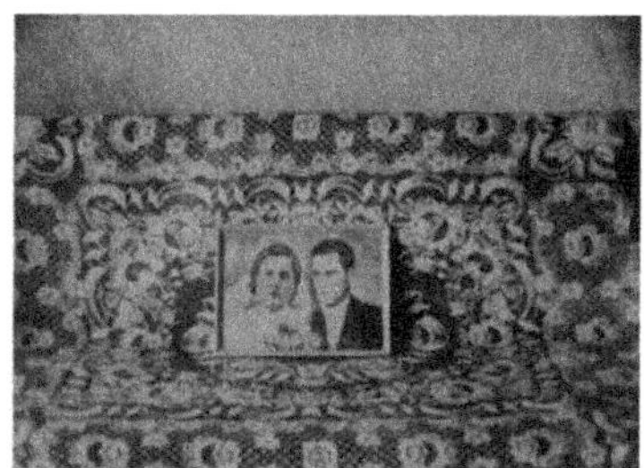

> *… one is photographable, 'photogenic',*
> *and this is perhaps the catastrophe,*
> *that one can be photographable,*
> *that one can be captured*
> *and caught in time …*
>
> ~ Hubertus von Amelunxen

… the tragedy of the photographic object, the object that is photographed: that in order to preserve its writing — the writing of light — the object has to be consigned into the shadows of time. Perhaps then, the only hope for the one being captured is to be photographed without being photographable: not so much that one is not in the photograph (that would be too simple), nor that one is the photographer (too banal), nor even that one attempts to resist being objectified (this being impossible); but that one remains within the photograph … as light.

Where one is nothing other than light writing itself.

Which is not to say that just because it is light it leaves no marks: for, no matter how light it might be, might try to be, there is always already weight, a mark made, an impression, a trace. And, this perhaps is precisely why it is the *unbearable lightness of being*: not because one has to try hard to weigh it down, give it *gravitas*, meaning even, but that no matter how light it is, regardless of the very *abgrund* of being, it is always already too heavy, never light enough.

Unless, it is light writing light.

And what remains is not just nothing — in the sense of light writing over itself — but nothingness: pure shining.

Perhaps completely *naïve* …

... but, I'm an absolute beginner;
with nothing much at stake.

~ David Bowie

[VIII]

46

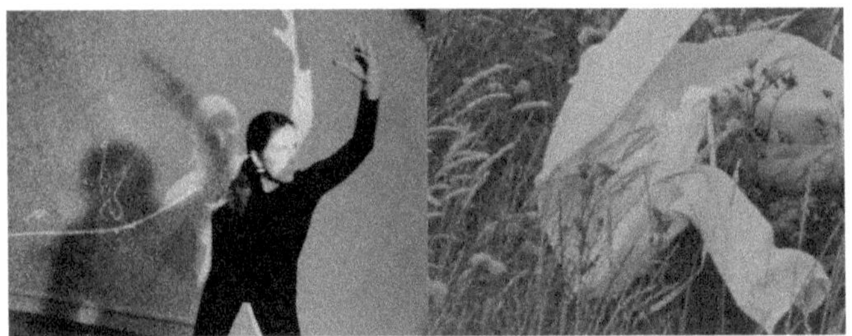

You said to me

if loss was a currency you'd be rich
but loss is a country and you were poor

a devastatingly beautiful line; one which, cuts is not quite the word but, certainly inscribes … wounds as well, leaves a mark, a note, perhaps even *une remarque,* there might always be music, it certainly tunes us a certain way, maybe even attunes us, sometimes detunes us, hopefully not into an episode of the *Looney Tunes.*

Bearing in mind — even as this might always be a burden on us — the beautiful, moving, beautifully-moving, movingly-beautiful, reminder of Jacques Derrida that « to have a friend, to look at him, to follow him with your eyes, to admire him in friendship, is to know in a more intense way, already injured, always insistent, and more and more unforgettable, that one of the two of you will inevitably see the other die ».

elle aussi, mon ami
toujours elle aussi

That, as he continues to teach us — with a lesson that could perhaps only reach us when he was gone (though, if we are reading him, is he truly gone; yes he is, no matter what we would like to think) that as the JD whom we read (but where there is no longer a 'who') — remains to teach us, the limit of friendship, when the friend is no longer with you (at least in person), is also its very condition.

That, without the risk not of death — which is not so much a risk as an inevitability — but the *risk of loss,* of being the one who is unfortunate enough not to have died, of being the one without the other whom one calls, has called, might always call, one's friend, there is no possibility of friendship itself.

But here, one should bear in mind — some burdens we will never be rid of, though one might ask if we are even trying to, intending to, (perhaps it is weight which weighs us down that also keeps us grounded, gives us grounding, a certain *grund*, even *gravitas*, no matter how fictive, to speak from) — one should try not to forget the fact that everyone dies twice:

> once bodily;
> the other time, when one is forgotten.

One would like to think the two sequential, but for those of us who are less fortunate, one can well be forgotten long before one is dead.

One can well be erased.

Cut.

Snipped.

Left on the floor of some editing suite.

> *How I wish, how I wish you were here*
> *We're just two lost souls*
> *Swimming in a fish bowl*
> *Year after year*
> *Running over the same old ground*
> *What have we found?*
> *The same old fears*
> *Wish you were here*
>
> ~ Pink Floyd

Your name.

Your name I shall hold on to.

Helena

> Oh Helena
> *our light*
>
> No wonder unphotographable,
> refusing to be captured in light
> for how does light write onto light
>
> He-Lena
> always already separable from the 'he'
> any 'he', shining alone
> a beacon in the dark
>
> And sometimes when we need a little chuckle,
> as we all do, our
> *he he he lena*
>
> H, oh H
> oh Helena,
>
> 3 steps on our ladder
> to writing
>
> and writhing

Names, all that be left behind to call — lovingly, angrily, frustratedly, longingly, pleadingly — to call out, to call to, when the other is gone.

Where perhaps the moment someone tells you their name, they are always already preparing you for the moment when there is nothing left to call but their name.

I hope you do too.

[IX]

50

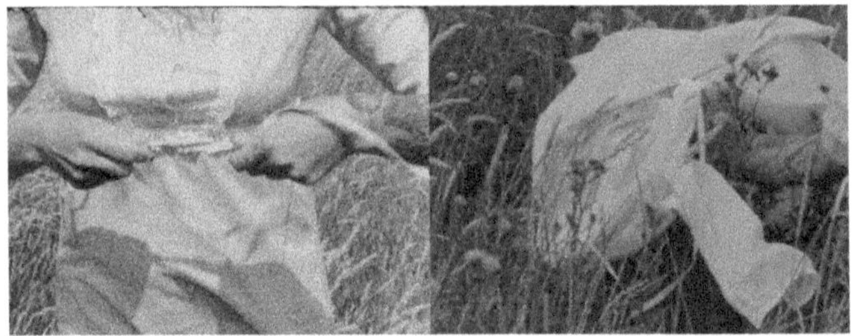

Oui, c'était une été admirable. Le souvenir en est plus fort que nous qui le portons … que vous, que vous et moi ensemble devant lui … c'était un été plus fort que nous, plus fort que notre force, que nous, plus bleu que toi, plus avant que notre beauté, que mon corps, plus doux que cette peau sur la mienne sous le soleil, que cette bouche que je ne connais pas.

~ Marguerite Duras[9]

And what can I tell you my brother, my killer
What can I possibly say?
I guess that I miss you, I guess I forgive you
I'm glad you stood in my way

~ Leonard Cohen

---

[9] *Yes, it was a wonderful summer. The memory of it is stronger than we who carry it … than you, than you and I together before it … it was a summer stronger than us, stronger than our strength, than us, bluer than you, more forward than our beauty, than my body, softer than this skin on mine under the sun, than this mouth that I do not know.*

~ Marguerite Duras

[X]

52

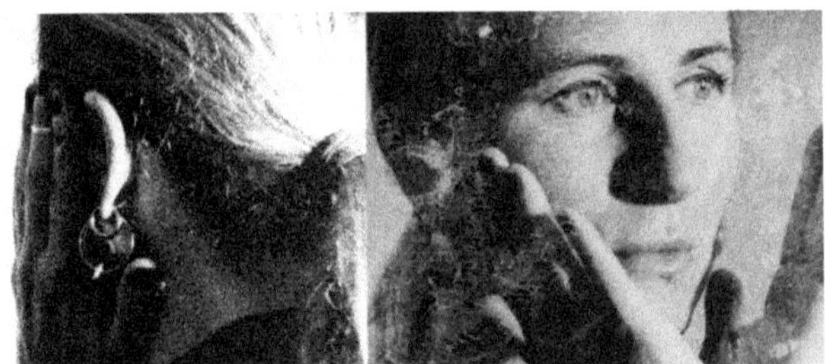

If I lose half my sight,
will my vision be halved?

~ Derek Jarman

If I can only see you, see your face, in half of the screen, do I only see half of you. Or 2 of you, just from different directions.

The blood of sensibility is blue

I consecrate myself

To find its most perfect expression

Whilst trying not to forget that what is sacred
always also keeps its secrets.

And makes us tremble, as it should.

Mysterium tremendum

For even if given to us, we don't always like what we get, even if it is good for us, perhaps especially when it be: after all, one is often *taught a good lesson by being given a good thrashing.*

But it is not as if I can really stop myself from following you. And looking into your eyes.

My pen chased this story across the page
tossed this way and that in the storm.

She'll tease you, she'll unease you
All the better just to please you
She's precocious, and she knows just what it
Takes to make a pro blush
All the boys think she's a spy, she's got Bette Davis eyes

~ Kim Carnes

The eye is simply a recorder, without or without our will.
Perhaps the same can be said of the heart.

~ Maggie Nelson

Your hands, touching your face. Your face, touching your hands. What do they say to each other, maybe only your ears hear.

And only here.

Like — or maybe only because I would like it to be — like how only your fingers, dear reader, might hear, as you read, what the page is rustling to you, as the page might have been the only one to hear the whispers of the reed.

I wonder how many people I've looked at all my life
and never seen.

~ John Steinbeck

[XI]

55

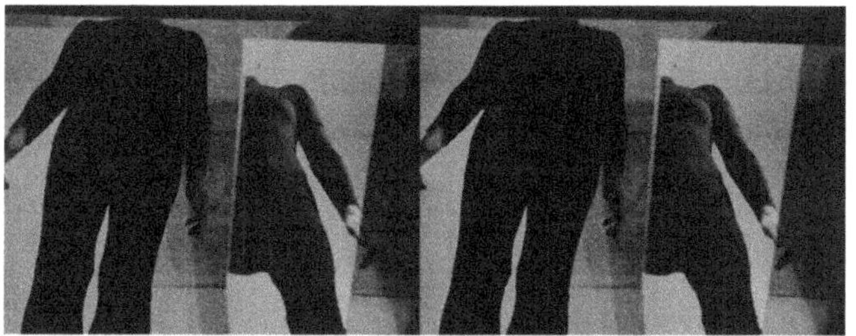

*We exist solely in the intermittence of our being, and that
what we call 'I' is just a shadow continuously bidding farewell
and saying hello, barely mindful of its own dissipation.*

~ Giorgio Agamben

My skin tells me where my body is

When it splits, when it bleeds — it writes me in the sheets
into the streets. Where her body is, where his body lies —
they split me in, spit me into, the streets
and I sink into my sheets

Writing with white ink —
you who so good with words

It isn't always what it seems when you're face to face with me
Not that we can see what you say, read what you writhe

Sometimes weird is pretty
Sometimes words are pretty
Never meant to cause you sorrow, bring you any pain
Even as I felt I might be drowning in my paint.

We can never look away
oh, we'll never look away
Under the shadow is where we'll stay
Under the shadow where we can play

> *'My' — what does this word designate?*
> *Not what belongs to me,*
> *but what I belong to,*
> *what contains my whole being,*
> *which is mine insofar as I belong to it.*

~Søren Kierkegaard

Many have come and gone. And yet I think you'll stay —
even when you've gone. In late night texts. Godforsaken snacks.
Unbridled sex

Maybe we'll live together in a photograph of time. No one is going to
take me away from you — there's no one left to take

If only I could see your face again once more. Your hair upon my
pillow like a slippery summer storm. Not that it'll pull me from the
wreckage of my silent reverie.

I let my guard down, thought that we would engage

At times am filled with rage — a fistful of love
invaded by a feeling

There's always some reason to feel not good enough
our bodies don't forget. Times I want to call you, but I won't let myself
regret you once felt like home.

All my secrets buried in my skin

Does the pain outweigh the pride?
Maybe tonight.

Sometimes words are pretty
Sometimes weird is pretty
Even as I swore as I was drowning in my paint
Never meant to cause you sorrow, any pain

We can never look away
oh, we'll never look away
Under the shadow where we can play
Under the shadow is where we'll stay

I love crowds. And their insincerity, their impersonality
They let me feel alone — let me be part of them
and apart from them

We can never look away
oh, we'll never look away
Under the shadow where we can play
Under the shadow is where we'll stay

My, my, my Delilah
Why, why, why Delilah

~ Tom Jones

Every day I think still of you
But maybe you'd rather not hear me
singing pretty lines. Humming rhymes
Writing weird lines

I like methinks singers who close their eyes —
playing not to the crowd be they
My lines, I take from everywhere but they don't make them
any less mine

Sometimes weird is pretty
Sometimes words are pretty
Only seemed to have caused you sorrow, to have brought you pain
Even though I'd never drown you in my paint

We can never look away
oh, we'll never look away
Under the shadow is where we'll stay
Under the shadow where we can play

> *Loneliness is still time
> spent with the world.*
>
> ~ Cheryl Charli

[XII]

60

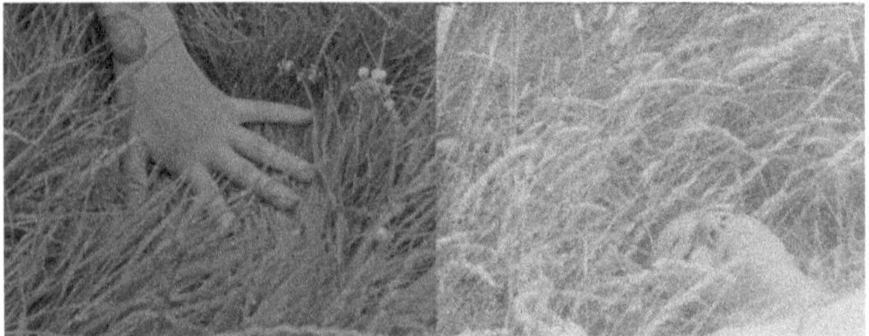

Jeremy Fernando

Le temps ne coule incolore
qu'à température ambiante

~ Pierre Alferi[10]

Green[11] | Grey[12]

Once you've accepted total obscurity,
you may as well do what you want.

~ Chris Kraus

---

[10] *Time flows colourless*
   only at room temperature

   ~ Pierre Alferi

[11] *Down the road I look and there runs Mary*
   Hair of gold and lips like cherries
   It's good to touch the green, green grass of home

   Yes, they'll all come to meet me
   Arms reaching, smiling sweetly
   It's good to touch the green, green grass of home

   /

   Yes, they'll all come to see me
   In the shade of that old oak tree
   As they lay me
   'Neath the green, green grass of home

   ~ Jerry Lee Lewis

[12] *I am very fond of footnotes at the bottom of the page, even if I don't have*
   anything in particular to clarify there.

   ~ Georges Perec

[XIII]

62

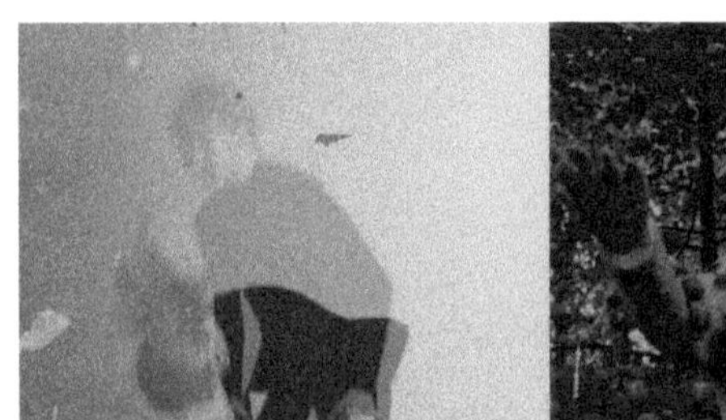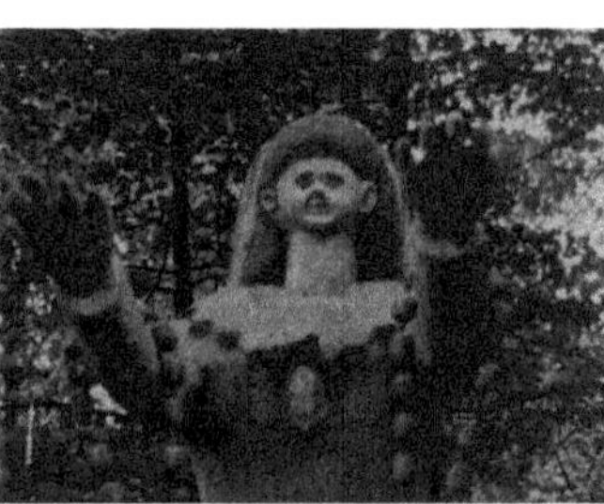

> *The truth is there is no 'because'. And because there is*
> *no 'because', there is also no 'why'. He did what he did.*
> *Sometimes things happen that way.*

~ Tash Aw

What did you do?
Your hands, exasperated, grasping your knees: *tell me, tell me*, you seem
to be saying.

> *The whole art is to know how to disappear before dying and*
> *instead of dying. I would say that part of disappearing is to*
> *disappear before you die, to disappear before you have run dry,*
> *while you still have more to say.*

~ Jean Baudrillard

Frozen into a smile,
hands almost akimbo. Gesturing, seeking,

> and we haven't even gotten to
> *why? as in why did you do what you did?*

> *If I could turn the page*
> *In time then I'd rearrange just a day or two*
> *Close my, close my, close my eyes*
> *But I couldn't find a way*
> *So I'll settle for one day to believe in you*
> *Tell me, tell me, tell me lies*
> *Tell me lies, tell me sweet little lies*
> *Tell me lies*
> *Tell me, tell me lies*

~ Fleetwood Mac

However, it is not as if anything, let alone everything, actually goes away. For,

> *nothing just vanishes; of everything that disappears there*
> *remains traces. The problem is what remains when everything*
> *has disappeared. It's a bit like Lewis Carroll's Cheshire Cat,*
> *whose grin still hovers in the air after the rest of him has*
> *vanished … Now, a cat's grin is already something terrifying,*
> *but the grin without the cat is something even more terrifying …*

~ Jean Baudrillard

Where both can really only say,
I wish I was there.

> *To write is to make oneself*
> *the echo of what cannot stop talking.*

~ Maurice Blanchot

[XIV]

65

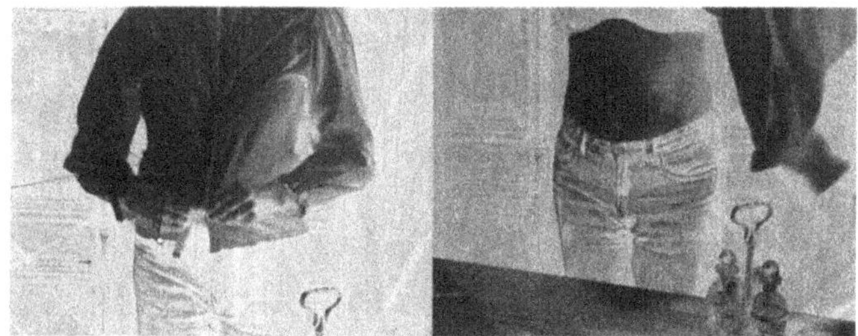

C'est beau
De ne pas savoir d'où viennent les choses
Les enchaînements secrets
Sont plus fins
Il est des intrigues
Au milieu desquelles on oublie
Le début, n'attend plus la fin
Quelques instants encore
Tout peut tout pénétrer.

~ Pierre Alferi[13]

Humans project onto ghosts
what they secretly fear about themselves.

~ Pan Huiting

Things,
they keep their secrets

~ Heraclitus

---

[13] *It is beautiful*
Not knowing from where things come
The secret sequences
Are more fine
There are intrigues
In the midst of which we forget
The beginning, no longer awaiting the end
A few more moments
Everything can penetrate all.

~ Pierre Alferi

[XV]

67

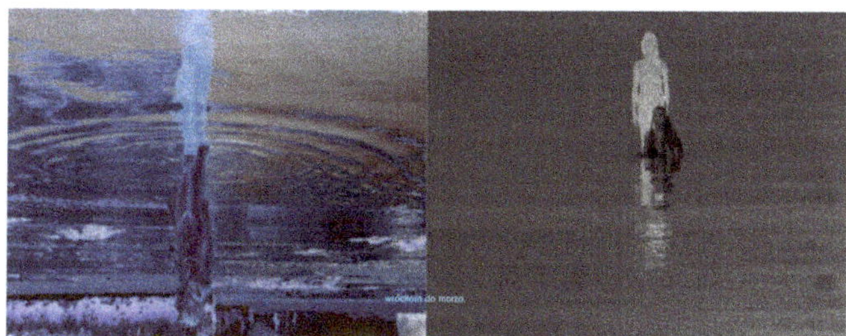

For Blue there are no boundaries or solutions.

Time is what keeps the light from reaching us.

*How did my friends cross the cobalt river, with what
did they pay the ferryman?*

~ Derek Jarman

*The 'I' narrating is me and you and the space between us.
We are the haunting and the haunted longing for something
and moving between secret (after)lives.
Ghosts are a state of being.*

~ Nate Lippens

In the roaring waters

I hear the voices of dead friends

Love is life that lasts forever

~ Derek Jarman

End Credits

A story by Helena Kuc as inherited by Kamila Kuc

An inheritance.

Not just that it was passed to, and through, you … but that, in some way, you also had no choice, that it was something handed-onto you, perhaps even placed-on[14] you; in some way, that is always going to be the *burden* of what comes before us: both by way of weight, what might weigh us down, and also of what is *borne* from us.

Not every gift is necessarily — or fully — wanted.

Perhaps just embraced:
after which it writes onto us.

> *Instead of asking ourselves how long it takes for a wound to heal, it would be better to ask: How long does it take for a wound to form? And how a wound can take a lifetime.*
>
> ~ Lucía Sbardella

> *We need a new word*
> *for what happens.*
> *It doesn't feel right*
> *just to call it real.*
>
> ~ Robert Kelly

---

[13] And, if you are once again hearing echoes of *place* — and not just that
of space, of geography, of *terroir,* but that of *placements,* of *being
in the right place,* and along with that, their companions★; of
replacements, perhaps even the fear of *being replaced* — you wouldn't be
just hearing voices in your head.

At least not just.

★ perhaps there is always bread, *panis,* involved

Trauma structures us,
so hold on to it.

~ Avital Ronell

But,

if you want to read, jump —
don't set yourself so much as a comma

~ Hélène Cixous

And, as for me,
quod scripsi scripsi.

The so-called political-film has often seemed to me to have something Wagnerian about it, to produce the same effects Wagner inspired in Nietzsche: you recognise it as powerful but feel it is artificial, ponderous …

~ Roland Barthes

Existence is not dialectical, not representable.
It is hardly liveable!

~ Félix Guattari

Neither painting nor drawing, nor art in general, can achieve anything. It is far removed from colonial appetites and does not even wish to beguile one's contemplation: art does not serve and there are no correspondences, intercessions, or contradictions to be found. This painting, this drawing, is entirely autonomous and engrosses the viewer in a vain search for analogies.

~ Hubertus von Amelunxen

WHERE YOU BELONG, I STILL WANDER
Kamila Kuc

I have moved all my books around and I still cannot write
this essay.

My act of remembering you, Helena, my grandmother, is an
attempt at holding onto a memory of my childhood and the
house at the edge of a forest. The house is still there, it now
belongs to my uncle, and the forest…It seems so much smaller
than the forest of my childhood. I understood why my father
needed to let go of the house. Every time we went to the
village, my child self now an adult, I saw a different father. He'd
become more tense, irritable, so short fused and critical of
everything and everyone.

Avital Ronell's words on *holding onto a trauma as a force that
shapes us* resonate deeply, though I resist being trapped in
trauma porn.

I watched the film last night.

I was there again. Before falling asleep on an airbed, nothing else
to do, reading seemed too demanding 48 hours before getting
on a plane to Seattle, my new home. 23 years of life in London.
Puff! Just like that I am moving. I am looking around this
empty three-storey town house. All this empty space. You lived
in two rooms your entire life. But you had the forest behind
you. And the farm ahead. I am moving to Seattle to be closer
to nature. 'Poland has plenty of nature' my father tells me in a

certain tone that I know is there because he is sad about me moving so far away. Perhaps I should have just moved to your village. *I should have bought your house.*

I can still see you, sitting on a bench in front of it. Peeling potatoes. Fast hands, sharp knife, no potato skin ever breaking, making endless swirls. I was mesmerised as a child. Perhaps this was my first encounter with art. Years later, it was a hot summer. I was supposed to be in the village for a week. I stayed for five, I didn't want to leave when my father suddenly showed up and said it was time to leave; your mother wants to see you, you leave for London next week, what were you thinking and what not. My phone off all this time, your landline barely working. I enjoyed being in my childhood, my parents driving me over every summer after school ended, leaving me behind for weeks. My bags were packed days before. The disappointment upon seeing my parents coming to take me back home always puzzled them. I must have already been confused as to where home was. Back in our small town I missed my tree houses. And the animals. I guess I also missed the thrill of your husband, my grandfather, running around the farm with an axe, terrorizing everyone after having one too many. I found it exciting, until I got older and wanted to attack him myself. I must admit I wasn't even thinking about defending you but mostly of all the animals he killed; the German shepherd whose head he cut off in the forest but brought back home for his own version of show-and-tell, the dogs he kept on tight chains, all the kittens he drowned. It wasn't just him. All the men around him were alike. Tormented by the wars, never having recovered from all the losses, living with the pain they couldn't really speak of. There was no language for it. The minute I start wondering about it, I want to drown Ronell's words in the ocean.

I was glad you and I had that last summer. You lived for two more summers but that was the last summer I saw you and the last time I saw you on your land. But the very last time we spent time together was in winter. The winter before you died. My parents brought you to their apartment; my mother was convinced this would be your last winter because your eyes turned pale blue and all watery. She was off by one winter. Last conversation you and I had on the phone was about rose jam doughnuts.

✳

This film made me realise I've never seen you smile.

Or is it that I just don't remember it? Selective memory discards events that are apparently less significant and I wonder what my selective memory is motivated by. Fucking amygdala. Still, I don't remember you ever smiling. The pictures prove that, too. There was an old VHS tape of my first, and last, communion. Some time in May 1990, or maybe 1991. You sit at a table next to my other grandparents. Everyone is laughing but you and Emil, my maternal grandfather. He was always sad. My first communion will soon be committed to its own proper spiritual death, a complete erasure with the Freddie Mercury Wembley Tribute concert. I've always liked that my parents didn't care so much that we taped over my first communion. Frankly, I was grateful for that, I hated my secondhand dress and that stupid nervous smile I had on my face when I knew I was being videoed (the irony of my future profession and my presence in this film is not lost). I watched that Freddie Mercury Tribute concert with my father over and over again. The tape got so worn out that it was unwatchable in parts, you had to fast forward, I think around the time INXS came on. I Iold that image... Later on, when editing this essay, Jeremy pointed out that INXS did not in fact play at that concert. Yet the image of Michael Hutchence standing on that Wembley stage is so present in my memory. Either way, just before the tape cuts to the concert, the last image, what's left of my first communion, is my brother, running around with a toy machine gun, chasing our cousin. Then a close up on you, looking into the space, somewhat petrified. I think children annoyed you. Laughter annoyed you. Or maybe the game of guns was simply too much.

> *If I am not writing, I am thinking about writing.*
> *I am composing. Recording movements.*
>
> ~ Therese Hak Kyung Cha, *Dictee*

My film is a series of movements of a body attempting to make sense of what came before it.

Though I may not remember you smiling, I know you took joy in digging potatoes, seeing gooseberries in your garden; little things you'd say, like the sun was good today. And then you'd make me a sandwich from your own moon-shaped bread, with your own butter and cottage cheese from your beloved cow that you taught me how to milk, even though I had no interest in doing so. I was too scared that the cow would kick me. She had a temper. In fact, you were the only person who could milk that cow. The cow was as feisty as you were. You often said that you and the cow were like sisters. She was also a custodian of your modest fortune; underneath her feet was a glass jar of money, your life savings, buried in the dry grass and cow shit. Every time my grandfather tried to get near the glass jar, the cow would make noises, which sent me into giggling fits. You wept a lot when you had to sell the cow because you ran out of money to feed your children. I always remembered you getting up at 4.30 every morning to feed the cow. You fed all your animals before you ate yourself and you never ate much, anyway, and you weren't really the greatest cook, either. That's an understatement. Though your bread, butter and cottage cheese were really out of this world.

When Ecka and I showed the film to a few of our Eastern European women friends, they all saw their own grandmothers in you. You became a symbol, but I am not sure that that's flattering, given the circumstances.

I don't remember which side of the frame I enter from.

Nevertheless, I insert myself into your story. Actually, I am in your story already, I have been in your story since I was born. I have become part of your story and you have become part of mine. Our lives seemingly so apart, I am well-aware of my inheritance and how similar we are.

Packing my stuff for Seattle. I am crossing the Atlantic without a single image of you. At least not in print. Only that wedding portrait of you and your husband that's in the film. I have a physical copy of this wedding portrait at my parents' apartment in Poland. It currently belongs to my father's brother. I object to that very fact but I guess the portrait came with the house. I have been searching for an artist who can make an accurate copy from its fragile original, or else, I am hoping that my uncle forgets I've ever had it. My mother mocked me for wanting to bring that portrait with me to Seattle, alongside the equally fragile portrait of the equally fragile marriage of her own parents. It really pissed me off, some things that she said to me that evening, off-handedly but perhaps she wanted me to have a fresh start.

I miss my books but they are neatly packed and on a boat to Seattle, my AirTag shows that they are circling somewhere near Hamburg right now. They've been there for weeks and what if they never get here and from now on I will have to write from memory. Plus, there are always too many diversions when one writes.

You are the centre of my film yet you are a spectre in it. Despite being quite stage-averse, I felt the need to write this film with my own body. I wanted my body to be in it as you reclaimed yours only after his death. Someone told me that I should refrain from nudity as the film may not play at festivals. Fuck that I thought and besides, Ecka's cello is something else altogether! The nudity is a non-image, it's a state of mind. Stripped bare. Without anything, like a country filled with loss. Bhanu Kapil's words: 'Some bodies don't somatize'. A few weeks before leaving London for Seattle I attended a Trauma Release Exercise workshop at a local yoga studio. I didn't get the shakes. I wanted to break down. I wanted to experience this masochistic collapse that my Freudian therapist so emotively warned me about for years. I should just resign myself to the fact that I am much better at making sense of anything once I've filmed it.

The body as a territory. A demarcation, of sorts. I had to ask you not to move your body when I was recording our conversation that last summer. The microphone bothered you, stuck to your chest like an intruder you had no reference for. You were good at school, but you couldn't continue because your father was killed and somebody had to help feed the family. You were the oldest. Back when you were able to go to school it'd take you a whole day to walk there and back. It would be the early evening by the time you were back and that simply took too much time. But you didn't mind learning the farm and you did so, beautifully. The farm became your life whereas for him it was a chore. This is where he lost, really. You loved the land and the land loved you back. He didn't have any of that. I think he was envious of it.

That first winter when you stayed at my parents' house, a few weeks after you were attacked by an intruder, your face to the ground, your house burgled … You walked from one window to the next, looking out of the 4th floor; our small town was a metropolis to you yet you were trapped in that box of an apartment. Twice a week my brother would visit and take you out for walks. You were dressed up and ready, sitting on a stool by the front door, listening for the sound of his car's engine, even though your hearing was weak. It was an innate instinct. The happiest I've seen you ever was when spring came and you were able to return to your land. This feeling of dislocation wasn't just about the physical space; your land was where you belonged, existentially. I always envied you this certainty. You knew your place in the world and this gave you strength.

That small village, such a volatile territory of your childhood, Poland's land contested for hundreds of years. We have not yet learned how to share land. Sepultura's 'war for territory' rings in my ears. I played this cassette on my tape player that I brought with me. It was somewhere around 1993 and I was caught between childhood and adolescence, still spending every summer in the village but fantasizing about the bigger world out there. My body akin to Homi Bhabha's unhomeliness – a certain psychological and cultural dislocation inherent to migration, even if out of choice.

I always loved that we could sit in silence together.

In this silence, I would often look at your hands. So small. So strong. The hands that worked the land, the hands that milked the cow, the hands that dug out potatoes. The hands that have never seen nail polish, not that it means anything but I am just saying that because half of my fridge is full of nail polish (and Super8 film). You certainly gave a good handshake that could squeeze a few tears out of the strongest of men.

Ecka and I have been talking about time in women's life. A morning conversation for me and an evening one for her. In my film there is no chronology, no need to adhere to any time. I swim in your story and I am aware of the word pun here, since you've never been to the sea. It drives me up the wall to know this yet I don't think you gave a shit.

There is a lot of blackness in the film.

You never wore black, even after he died you never wore black and yet, you were so devoted to the church and its rituals. You didn't want to die. You only really started living after his passing. I think that deep down you didn't believe that the church was going to save you.

You appeared in my dream recently.

In this dream you speak very clearly and you tell me that I should shop in Sprouts. I am going to ignore the fact that you spoke in English because that just blows my mind. You never shopped in a supermarket yourself, instead, a mobile store came to the village every week. You'd wait by the side of the road in fear of missing it. In Seattle, I overstock on food. I have been overstocking on food my entire life. It drove all my partners crazy. I guess I've been, somewhat clumsily, trying to overcome some old imaginaries; some form of poverty of means, which is what this film is: cinematographer, sound artist and I. And a lot of favours. We are so much closer to your reality this way. My own *dépays*, this familiar and somewhat comfortable feeling of displacement is also this confusion I've been experiencing, this tension between my origins — i.e. the house at the edge of the forest, and the new direction I am heading in — a-more-than-comfortable middle-class life, further and further away from the house at the edge of the forest. I still envy you your certainty of where you belonged.

Despite all of that other stuff, all the other stories.

A body can be destroyed by a story.

A body can become a story.

It can become still.

You were barely ever still. You only became still that winter when you started getting weaker and my parents decided that you had to live with them, miles away from your home, from your land, yet safer.

I spend a fair bit of time in *shavasana*, known as a corpse pose yet it is there that I am so acutely aware of just how alive I am; how much I am breathing. Last few hours of your life were agony, you ran out of oxygen. You woke up in the middle of the night, all sweaty and hot, you ran out into your front yard and ripped your nightgown off before surrendering to stillness. That same nightgown that is now an artefact in my film, a silent witness.

Your body, this powerful instrument of resistance... To narrate it, to put it in a box of linearity that narrative often requires was always to be a futile task. A body can change the course of a story. I am now in Seattle. I am pondering Sara Ahmed's migrant orientation. Me — the subject on the move, looks simultaneously backward to previous, past locations that no longer exist and forward to places that are not yet home. Your house in the village — it no longer exists as I experienced it. You are not there. Seattle is not quite home yet.

You died in the middle of the pandemic, on the night I finished editing my feature, which ends with your words. These words you shared with me that summer I recorded our conversation; the summer my father and I argued viciously about what I should be doing with my life. I love him. He's always been a good father. We always patch it up. We had a version of this argument recently, a month before I moved to Seattle. We made peace again. I lay in his arms, crying quietly as he is stroking my hair. We love each other deeply which is why we argue so hard, he says.

In May Ecka and I went to Hoylake.

We stayed at her mother's house. We came here to record sound for the film. Before we did anything, I'd venture out for a morning swim and a beach run in such thick fog that a couple of times I could not find my way back home.

There it is again.

Home.

Ecka's mother's home. Her house. Not my home though I felt very comfortable in Hoylake. Every time I find myself in a new place I often wonder: could I live here? The answer is usually yes, which some find troubling. Restlessness, some twisted desire for nomadism? It's hard to be a nomad with 3000 books, three surfboards, and a cat. Maybe I have displaced my feelings of displacement. *I was there / was I there? / who was there? / who was where?* Nevertheless I now can't ignore the fact that there is always an image of a house in every Tarot reading I've ever done. In Hoylake doing our Tarot cards became our daily practice, three cards a day for each one of us. Something to do as our friendship blossomed. Later in the day we'd go to the beach and record sound. I'd walk on razor clam shells; we arranged them carefully to get the best sound.

I am not even sure whether we used them in the final film. We would play Ecka's mother's meditation bells before a knock on the door appeared. A speedy order of Super 8 film arrived from London, because I got an idea for a new film. Ecka, Louis, and myself are on that beach again; creative energies coming together without a plan: 'The time is now. The location is the North Sea — the sea beaten into submission by the descending sun; and the beach that looks like a desert.'

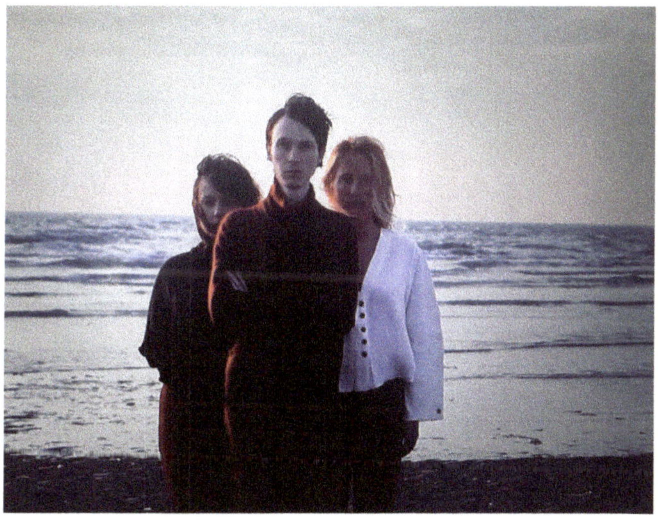

WRITING TIME

Jeremy Fernando

> *The idea that a writer should be contemporaneous is itself modern,*
> *but I should say it belongs more to journalism than to literature.*
> *No real writer tried to be contemporary.*
>
> ~ Jorge Luis Borges[1]

When is it time to stop reading and start writing?

A question I hear all the time, particularly when someone catches-on that you do some writing; right after the moment someone spies you scribbling things down at a bar, café, restaurant, in the park, on the bus, in a tram, while riding a train, in a book that you are reading, especially in a book you are reading.

It's almost as if one has to be surreptitious when you are writing.

But not because you are actually doing anything, for *literature itself is fundamentally useless.*[2]

---

[1] Jorge Luis Borges, *On Writing*, edited and translated by Norman Thomas de Giovanni, Daniel Halpern, & Frank MacShane. Hopewell: The Ecco Press, 1994, 53.

[2] And here, the question of 'who gets to decide if something — a work, a piece of writing, a text — is literature?' arises. Is it something to be left to so-called experts: and what actually makes anyone (or any series of bodies) an expert in reading. Which is always also the question of *authority* and *power*: the difference between them being, the latter involves violence while the former has to be granted, and more specifically, by the ones who willingly come-under said figure. So, perhaps when it comes to literature, it is more a question of authority: for no one can actually compel you to accept that something is literature (perhaps only a teacher, who might do so using the violence of grades should you deign to disagree with them; but even then 'accepting under duress' is by no means agreement, so only a performative assent at best).

And since literature has to do with reading (at least hopefully it does) then perhaps the only one who can decide is the one who reads (*lit*). *Surtout dans un lit.*

Which is precisely why those in power have always been fearful of it: and we know that all too well from the histories that we read, in stories that inscribe themselves despite the resistances of those in power, in tales that leave marks to be read in spite of every effort made to erase them.

For, one should try never to forget that the first to be shot are almost always poets, writers, artists.

Not because they actually do anything, but that precisely by doing nothing they give — allowing all echoes of *gift* to resound here — they open, the space for us to imagine something else, something other. And by entwining literature with use, all that is done is to tie it down to, entwine it with, the state; all that is done is to diminish it, to enchain it to value, production, logic, ratio, reason.

Where if you listen carefully,
it is not too difficult to hear
le cri de l'écriture.

It is to do nothing other than to attempt to erase literature.

———————

Or, if Jacques Derrida is to be believed, a work is a work of literature when it is a text that is under erasure (*sous rature*) whilst being read (*lit*): that it foregrounds its own making as it is being read. Having its own case of 'archive fever' as it were.

Either way, naught to do with the one who writes.

In a different piece, so space — and time — we might have also opened the question of the difference between *someone who writes* and *an author*. (For the moment, let me slightly shamelessly — with a *mea culpa* — say that should you wish to consider the question, please feel free to read my 'On Afterwords; or, what comes after the word…' in Francisco Cândido Xavier, *Poetry from Beyond the Grave*, translated by Vitor Pequeno. The Hague: Uitgeverij, 2013: 193-232).

abandoned to freedom

two systems sounds fine
her handbag tightly clasped said deaf
to you abandoned

to freedom

fifty years divined
yet tremblingly umbrellas disappeared merely three
shy of two score

just so

spectres of one cannot we avert
yet each day wafts freedom unconfined
towards

uncharted skies

still open

And here we might ask the question, 'when does writing
become *writing*?'

Perhaps more precisely — as if precision was something we
were even aiming for (but it might still be important to keep
up pretenses; after all, one sometimes hopes one's inscriptions

get published; *daddy daddy please chose me*)[3] — okay, yes so, a more precise question might take the form of, 'when is the moment marks made *turn into*, *are seen as*, or even *are taken to be*, writing?'.

For we all know, somewhat instinctively, that there is a difference between *something written down* and *writing* (which is probably why we all balk at emails; are suspicious of *les communiqués*, one has good reason to be wary of anything reeking of the police; also why we should raise our eyebrows as anyone who calls themselves a writer).[4]

And, why do we consider writing in a diary, *journaling* — where time, *le jour*, takes place of pride over the fact of mark marking, even as it is the fact that being noted, marked, highlighted, underlined, is precisely what makes it stand-out from the rest of the day, where everything else is merely the remains of the day. Which also implies, or at least opens a possibility, that *writing* — if writing here is set in opposition to, or at least aside from, journaling — that writing is mark making divorced from the day, separated from time; that there is a certain *timelessness* to writing.

---

[3] The spectre of authority is very difficult to disperse, even after — maybe even especially after — the death of said figures. Just ask Hamlet Jr. Who, it must be said, made one of the best attempts by taking out a notepad and consigning daddy's request (command? plea?) into writing … transforming « remember me » into a mere reminder …

✳

And when one hears writing, if one listens carefully, one can also pick up on a certain writhing, a slipping, sliding, slithering, in, and with, language. And here, one might reopen speculation on the uncomfortable relationality between authority and authorship; and the writer having to sneak herself in, not just past the reader, but past herself as reader, her reading of herself.

~ Jeremy Fernando, *Writing Death*. The Hague, Uitgeverij, 2011, 52.

[4] You wouldn't be hearing things if you once again catch whispers of authority in this calling, in this *calling oneself* which is a form of self-summoning — or, more deliciously, in the Singlish as *ownself call ownself* (with its echoes of *ownership* resounding in the background; oh property and propriety be always involved).

That it is *quod scripsi scripsi* as it remains that way: that it is precisely what remains of the day because after *le jour* is gone, this is what stays forever, *pour toujours*.

Where there is a possibility that scribbling, inscription, becomes *writing* when there is a certain ossification.[5]

Where what Susan Sontag says of photography — « life is a movie, death is a photograph »[6] — might well be true of writing too.

Is this perhaps why journalists tend to be suspicious of writers: is there something more faithful involved in attempting to record the day than in writing one? Even if this *fidelity* relies on a faith in being able to attest to a day, to bear witness to it; perhaps, as importantly, to be able to lock down a moment into time.

> *Literature depends not just on the right to say anything*
> *but also on the right not to be held responsible for what one says*
>
> ~ J. Hillis Miller[7]

Je suis journaliste parce que j'écris le jour.

---

[5] So quite possibly, once again, a question of time.

[6] Susan Sontag, *The Benefactor*. New York: Farrar, Straus & Giroux, 1963, 177.

[7] J. Hillis Miller, 'What is Literature?' in *On Literature*. London: Routledge, 2002, 5.

As interestingly, Hillis attributes this observation, one might even say claim, to Jacques Derrida, which I'm quite sure was a homage to his old friend's insights and thought: at the same time (at the risk of being irresponsible to Hillis, with a *mea culpa* if I am being so★) attribution — citation being one of its manifestations — is also a form of disavowal … as if to say, *if you don't agree with me, take it up with JD* (or, in my case, JHM)

★in this case it might be completely apt though: for I first met Hillis at a conference entitled *Irresponsibility* … so a salutation, in fond fond memory, of our time together.

Or even more so: *je suis journaliste parce que je suis l'auteur des jours.*

So, when is it time to stop reading and start writing?

A question one hears all the time: as if *writing* and *reading* are separable — not that they are the same thing.

But that one can only know that writing has taken place by first reading.

Or, as Marguerite Duras would say, in a far more elegant way than I ever could, « *et lire, c'était écrire* »,[8] *and reading, it was to write.* So, not just that to read is to know there were writing, but that *reading itself is writing.* Which does open another, rather delicious, possibility: is the writing that happens as one reads one that is in-time, of-time; one in which ink has yet to dry.[9]

---

[8] Marguerite Duras, *Écrire*. Paris: Gallimard, 1993, 36.

L'écriture de la littérature, c'est celle qui pose un problème à chaque livre, à chaque écrivain, à chacun des livres de chaque écrivain. Et sans laquelle il n'y a pas d'écrivain, pas de livre, rien. Et de là, il semble qu'on puisse se dire aussi, que de ce fait-là, il n'y a peut-être plus rien.

~ Marguerite Duras, 'La mort du jeune aviateur anglais', dans *Écrire*, 82.

[9] For a meditation on the relationship between ink (*calmar*), calamari, reading, writing, love, and fidelity, please see my *in fidelity*. Singapore: Delere Press, 2016.

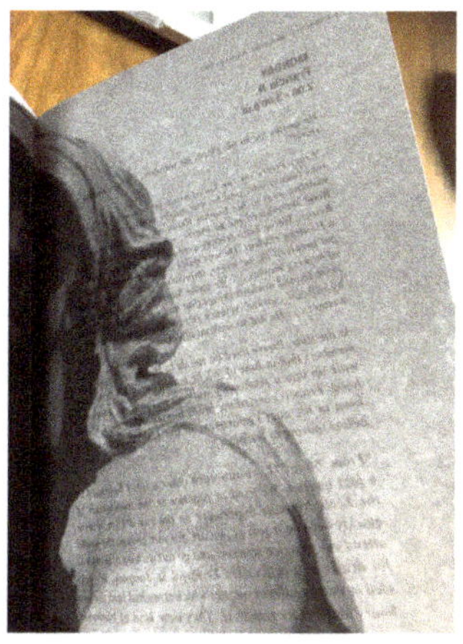

light | writing | time — through Sophie Calle, 2018

If you want to read, jump,
don't set yourself so much as a comma.

~ Hélène Cixous[10]

To read, perchance to dream,
'aye, there's the rub

---

[10] This was Hélène Cixous' response to my question, 'how do you read?' during my conversation over tea at her apartment in Paris in June 2017. Naturally, I neither recorded nor took notes during the afternoon (this was no 'interview', so that would have been rude) but from scribbles I made in a notebook later that evening; so from memory. And, regardless of what one calls that form of inscription, it would not be far-fetched to say that her phrase has *written itself into me.*

Sometimes whatever is written is strange, unfamiliar, other, to me — a fragment of me, sometimes it also fragments me. Like when I am reading, re-reading really, what I ostensibly have written here: it all seems slightly odd, as if it were the hand of someone else who had inscribed this text; and it might well have been another.[11]

> *The creation of an object: a real act of faith,*
> *taking place before my enchanted eyes.*
>
> ~ Henri Bosco[12]

Nor can I ever quite control how it will be read: I can only write, read, and leave it to be read.

And in the meantime …

The crucial element in all narrative, and in life. The difference being that in the latter, one is wholly unaware of what is

---

[11] Which opens the question: 'where does *editing* lie in the relationship between reading and writing?' One might posit that it might be the act (if it can be called an act; perhaps *moment*) wherein writing and reading occur concurrently: or, at least where both reading and writing are involved in every moment (*gesture?*) of editing.

> *eh dit : mais qui parle ?*

[12] Henri Bosco, *Le Jardin d'Hyacinthe*. Paris: Gallimard, 1946, 192 (as read in Gaston Bachelard, *The Poetics of Space*, translated by Maria Jolas. London: Penguin Classics, 2014, 88).

happening — even, perhaps especially, if it affects one, until much later, often when it is much too late.

Time can be very mean indeed.

> *Being completely alive is a task, it's not at all a given thing. It's not just about being present to the world, it's being present to yourself, reaching an intensity that is in itself a way of being reborn.*
>
> ~ Anne Dufourmantelle[13]

On July 21, 2017, Anne died whilst attempting to rescue two children caught in dangerously turbulent waters off Pampelonne beach in Ramatuelle. Lifeguards eventually reached the children, who survived; but she could not be resuscitated.

Risk, Anne never lets us forget, risk is an essential part of life, an integral part of living, of being alive.

As is living one's writing in time.

One day, as we were walking in the forests of Saas Fee, I turned to my dear teacher, Avital Ronell, and asked how to respond to a block in writing, to deal with the dreaded writer's block.

---

[13] Anne Dufourmantelle, 'The Ideology of Security', public lecture at The European Graduate School, (August 2011).

For a longer, beautiful, often deeply-moving, meditation on the relationship between *risk* and *living*, please read Anne Dufourmantelle, *Éloge du risque*. Paris: Éditions Payot & Rivages, 2011.

In her inimitable way, without missing a skip, she responded, almost in beat, rather in time with our steps, « perhaps you need to move your books around … ».[14]

Animate them to learn from them (*boccræft*, book learning), to open them, to open yourself to learning from them, being literate to them … perhaps writing begins when one *moves the ink* around again …[15]

Shaken. Stirred.

Whilst never forgetting that even as you might have been the one who has taken the books — off a shelf, from the bookstore, a library, from the interwebs — and laid them on your desk, bed, table, one's reasons for doing so and the those of the books themselves might not quite be the same: particularly if the register of sequence, relation, order of things, of words, *les choses avant les mots, ou même les choses sont les mots*, is opened.[16]

Where, even as animation might be taking place, who is animating what — or what is animating whom — remains a question that is quite possibly beyond one.

---

[14] A line that was said, and heard, in time … so one that has also disappeared into its winds … and now also into ink, and writing, *written into time.*

[15] *Ellipsis is the rhetorical equivalent of writing: it depletes, or decompletes, the whole so as to make conceptual totalities possible. And yet every conceivable whole achieved on the basis of ellipsis is stamped with the mark of the original loss.*

~ Werner Hamacher, 'Hermeneutical Ellipses: Writing the Hermeneutical Circle in Schleimacher' in *Premises: Essays in Philosophy and Literature from Kant to Celan.* Redwood City: Stanford University Press — Meridian, 1999, 74.

[16] In another life, this might have led us down the path to Michel Foucault and his work on *confession:* allowing us to open the question, 'is there a certain amount of torture involved in learning thoughts, ideas, notions, from texts'; after all, reading and thinking often involves probing, extracting, gleaning, questioning, grilling …

After all, as Nietzsche continues to remind us *movement and vitality is life*: as he teaches us, « this is the way in which religions are wont to die out: under the stern, intelligent eyes of an orthodox dogmatism, the mythical premises of a religion are systematized as a sum total of historical events; one begins apprehensively to defend the credibility of the myths, while at the same time one opposes any continuation of their natural vitality and growth; the feeling for myth perishes, and its place is taken by the claim of religion to historical foundations ».[17]

And who also tries to never let us forget that thinking often involves *throwing up*.

For, ideas can grip you, take a hold of you, *infect* you, cause inflections in you, sometimes even overwhelm you (whatever defenses you think you might have had) … where you run the risk of overheating.

Inseminate themselves into you … and carrying a thought to term — particularly when they are moving, shaking, dancing, kicking, screaming (*peut-être encore un cri de l'écriture*), writhing — can be very dangerous indeed.

Perhaps *to think*, to really chew on a thought, is to always also run the risk of *having a fever*.

Where perhaps their revenge involves writing themselves into our bodies: drilling themselves into our brains, our bones, our souls. Like in some penal colony.

The path — well, really my path (so this might be some confession of sorts) — always seems to lead to Octave Mirbeau and his garden.

[17] Friedrich Nietzsche, *The Birth of Tragedy*, translated by Walter Kaufmann. New York: Vintage Books, 1967, 75.

Sometimes, I dream of being able to just read and write,
and not have to bother about quotidian concerns like
rent, sustenance, being able to sustain myself. Least of all
employment or, perhaps even worse, book sales: it's a terrible
feeling when one is more concerned about whether people
are buying one's works than if said works are of interest to
anyone as works; that is the moment you turn a work into
a mere product, when writing becomes that most hated of
contemporary terms, content.

Sometimes, I dream of having a patron;
a boy can only dream.

> *There is also the courage of the writer who braves the kind of censorship
> that forbids 'insignificant' confidences.*
>
> ~ Gaston Bachelard [18]

But then, at the same time, one can't help but wonder if it
is possible to separate the patronage of your work from you
being patronised: moreover, after which there is certainly no
possibility of a free-hand, of emancipation … daddy will always
be holding your *manus*.

And your manuscript is always also going to bear the mark of
their signature: whether anyone one else can see this signing-
off, underwriting, crutch even, being a different, somewhat
irrelevant, question. Whenever you read your own script, you
will see their imprints … for all time … smudged all over it.

✳

---

[18] Gaston Bachelard, *The Poetics of Space*, 91.

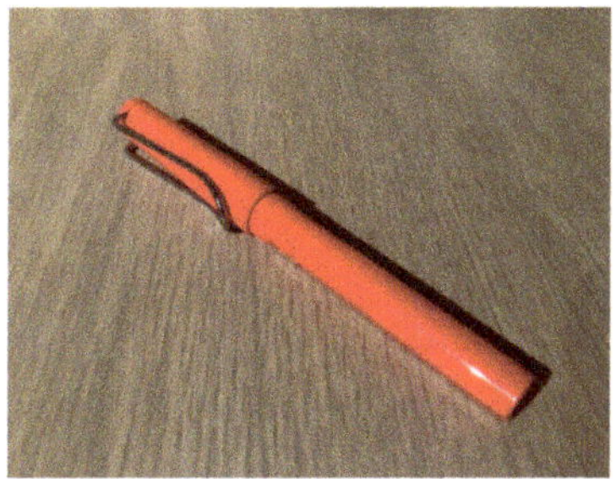

to writhe, perchance to dream, 2019

Each time I attempt to write, one of the sound-tracks I keep hearing, that I cannot get out of my mind, that plays on constant loop in the background, is that I were not good enough, that I should go somewhere else with what I was going to write, with what I had not even written — that I should just stop writing and take a hike, take your marks, movements, elsewhere, as it were.

After all, those of us who write constantly put ourselves before the law: even voluntarily submit ourselves to it — during the process of making our works, building our projects, writing essays, searching for grants, trying to land a book deal, trying to find some space within a magazine or a home in some journal — willingly sign some kind of masochistic contract. And also bind ourselves to a publishing industry, sometimes tied to a job market, certainly some sort of hierarchical, institutional system, where we are judged, timed, told to *first do your time,* unceasingly examined — but at the same time know not who judges us: so there is no recourse, no real possibility of any appeal, no statute of limitations, to the judgement.

Where this nameless, faceless, recourseless, judgement also potentially renders it into an unending — *timeless* — one.

And should one ever deign to raise a complaint, one is told that *this is the path you have chosen*, that you elected to *walk this walk*, that it is *this way or the highway*.

But still, regardless of the trials one might be facing on one's walks, one must also bear in mind that even as one is able to walk, to move around, to roam, there are many who can no longer walk, who no longer feel safe to walk, who are not allowed to walk. From much maligned indentured workers, whose walks, whose movements, are seen, constantly construed — vindictively, racially, perhaps even stupidly — as a threat; to civil-rights marches that are cordoned, shepherded, uncivilly beaten, violently attacked; to assemblies — in Buenos Aires, Beirut, Budapest, Caracas, Mexico City, Mariupol, New York, Oakland, London, Kiev, Hong Kong, Paris, Selma, Singapore, Taipei, Gaza, oh Gaza, amongst many many others — that are threatened, charged upon, deemed illegitimate, illegal, unsocial, unpatriotic, even irrelevant, brutally dispersed in order to make way for certain kinds of movement that are authorised, approved, sanctioned; to our lesbian, gay, bi-sexual, trans-gender, queer, intersex, asexual, friends whose drives, desires, bodies, are policed, criminalised, who are told to get behind, keep themselves behind closed doors, unable to walk in the open, to waltz in the sun, who are told that their attractions, their bodily passions, are beyond the pale; to *les desaparecidos*, whose very movements, ability to move, to walk, were literally disappeared, made to vanish from the streets, from our communities, who were separated from the lives of others, quite possibly from their very own; to refugees who are told that their presence is, their very footsteps on lands, are illegal, who are thrown into processing centres, treated as non-humans, kept barely alive, just *bare life*; to everyday occurrences where some people are, where one is, told to move faster, move slower, to get out of the way.

Which is not to say that one should ever ask, have to apply, for permission to walk, or to stop walking: after all, it is — at least should be — one's right to move, to walk. But that even as walking, moving, movement, and thinking, are related, have a relation with each other, this relationship can be coopted, swallowed, perhaps digested, turned back upon us — where instead of choosing to move, we are moved, shifted, shafted; where instead of thinking, we are herded, flocked, maneuvered, into unthinking.

Dream Sleep

ticktockticktocktick
tockticktockticktock
ticktockticktocktick
tockticktockticktock
ticktockticktocktick
tockticktockticktock
ticktockticktocktick
tockticktockticktock
tickcrosstickcrosstick
crosstickcrosstickcross
tickcrosstickcrosstick
crosstickcrosstickcross
tickcrosstickcrosstick
crosstickcrosstickcross

écrit.cri.écrit
cri. écrit. cri.

So, when is it time to stop reading and start writing?

Maybe never.

Rather to always read-write write-read … not because they are
the same thing, nor because reading would generate writing
(in many ways, that kind of calculativeness, writing with an
a prior purpose, is somehow worse, at least to me) … but that
in writing-reading reading-writing one can dream of the
possibility of the two crafts momentarily touching each other.

With *stopping* and *starting* it is always a question of *time*: which
is perhaps always also a question of the relationship between a
work and time.

For, when one speaks of works — especially if one is opening
the possibility that the work might move beyond itself, might
reach a level of craft that is *un pas au-delà*, a *step-beyond* and a
not-beyond itself at the very same time, if we were feeling a little
adventurous we might even say, the possibility that it becomes a
work of art — the echo of *timelessness* is never far from it; even
as, at the same time, no work can exist outside of time, outside
of its time. Which implies, as both my old teachers Giorgio
Agamben and Alain Badiou posit, at the point where a work
becomes art, at the moment when a work is recognised as art, it
is *both in and outside of time* — or perhaps even *with its own time*.[19]
Which might be why for something to be considered a work

---

[19] This notion of the relationship between art and time — through the contemporary,
with-time — was explored by both Agamben and Badiou at their respective seminars
at The European Graduate School, so at specific moments in time. Similar thoughts, for
they can never be the same (even if from the same person), in different times. Or,
perhaps two different times coming together, right now, over me … in writing, ah
writing, ossification (ah, bones*) … a setting in time again …

*it is probably no coincidence — of if it is, a beautiful confluence — that one of the
oldest form of writing is bone writing.

of art it has to *stand the test of time*: it has to be *contemporary*; even if it is always from *before the time* it is seen, and also seen too-soon, is *ahead of its time*. For, a work of art always already draws from what comes before; echoes memories of works past, works inscribed in, onto, into, it; harkens to, resounds with, a line, genealogy, of works it is a part of — and, at the same time, breaks from, breaks forth from, these works, strikes out on its own; stands apart from its lineage, is unfamiliar to the ones before, is perhaps even unrecognisable, *sui generis*, a stranger, or even just strange.[20]

Where, in the encounter between one and a work of art, what one is seeing is the *time of the work itself* — the time of the work being nothing other than another name for art. Which is not to say it is a separate time: of course not. Nor a mystical, divine, time: at least not necessarily so.

But that it is the *same time that is not the same*.

Or, as our Thai friends might say, in a far more elegant way: in a time that is *same same but different*.

---

[20] And here, in a different time — for, we probably have run out of space, thus time (one should never overstay one's welcome) — we would have opened the question of *hospitality*.

But, as a guest of dear Kamila, who so kindly invited me to respond to her beautiful *I was there*, the last thing I would want to do is turn into an *invader*.

twenty twenty-three

the only thing that
continues to surprise me
is that we are still

surprised that we still
continue to claim to be
surprised each time this

happens as if the
surprise would save us having
to acknowledge that

we would much rather
remain surprised than to not
devour prizes

peoples lands so *this*
is no doubt a perfectly
ordinary year [21]

I wake up in the morning and I wonder
why everything's the same as it was

~ Skeeter Davis [22]

---

[21] closing line to the poem '一九八九年' by Yang Lian, translated into the English as '1989'
by Brian Holton. Yang Lian taught at The European Graduate School as a guest at Judith
Balso's seminar, *Poetry & Philosophy*, in August 2005, where he also performed a reading
of this poem in the Mandarin as part of his evening lecture.

[22] Sylvia Dee & Arthur Kent, 'The End of the World', single by Skeeter Davis, New York:
RCA Victor, 1962.

It has taken me years to admit — perhaps only to myself — that
I don't care about writing something important, something
significant. That my only hope, wish — dream even — is to
write something beautiful …

… a boy can only dream …

And if you are wondering why so many quotations, citations,
echoes of the writings of others appear here, show–up in all my
writings, the only thing I can say is all of my thoughts, notions,
scribbles, inscriptions, come from elsewhere, and owe
a deep thanks to my teachers. For, I'd like to think that thinking
(*denken*) should always also entail thanking (*danken*).[23]

After all, friends have an effect on you, can sometimes open a question in you, might well affect you, unveil a new register, perhaps inseminate a thought in you, might even infect you — somedays, I dream that *my writing is syphilitic*; a boy can only dream.

And the gamble that is taken each time one looks at a work, picks up a text, the risk one runs in attempting to attend to it, to another, any other, is the possibility of *falling* — along with all the potential disasters this entails — of falling *in love*.[24]

> *Baby don't hurt me,*
> *don't hurt me, no more*
>
> ~ Haddaway[25]

Where, the stake in *writing*[26] is one's very own self.

---

[23] For this reminder, I would like to proffer thanks to my dear teacher, my dear dear friend, Avital Ronell.

[24] Love, which as Alain Badiou in conversation with Nicholas Truong reminds us, is « a construction, a life that is being made, no longer from the perspective of the One but from the perspective of Two » (29). However, this is not a fusing of two into one, the romantic notion that continues to haunt thinking of love, a notion that not only — as in classic mythology — leads towards death, but more importantly, leads to the effacement of one by another, an effacement of relation itself. Instead, this is love that « invents a new way of lasting in life … a new way of experiencing time » (23).

Alain Badiou with Nicholas Truong. *In Praise of Love*, translated by Peter Bush. London: Serpent's Tail, 2012.

[25] Dee Dee Halligan & Junior Torello, 'What is Love' in *The Album*. Cologne: Coconut Records, 1993.

It is always a challenge to the self, to our selves: it is a call to attend to the possibility of another, of something that is more important than us. That might be why love's such an « old fashioned word » as it « dares you to care for the people on streets, on the edge of the night … dares you to change our way of caring about ourselves » and that when you dare to care, when you attune yourself to the call of another, it might well be your « last dance » : all of this with a bow to Roger, John, Brian, Freddy, that is Queen, and David Bowie.[27]

And like any call, it might well lead us to dash ourselves on the rocks.

Herein lies its danger.

And its beauty.

---

[26] So, always also reading. But it did seem a little impolite to foreground the dangers of reading to a reader at the very moment they are doing so.

   That is, assuming there are any readers at all: perhaps this being one of the risks of writing — that one is never read. The other risk being that one is.

[27] Roger Taylor, Freddie Mercury, John Deacon, Brian May, & David Bowie, 'Under Pressure' in Queen, Hot Space. London: EMI Records, 1982.

He realised that every writer must be forgotten almost as soon as they have stopped writing, because the page had been lost, has literally flown away, has entered a context of different situations and sentiments, answers questions put by other men, which its author could not have even imagined.

~ Enrique Vila-Matas

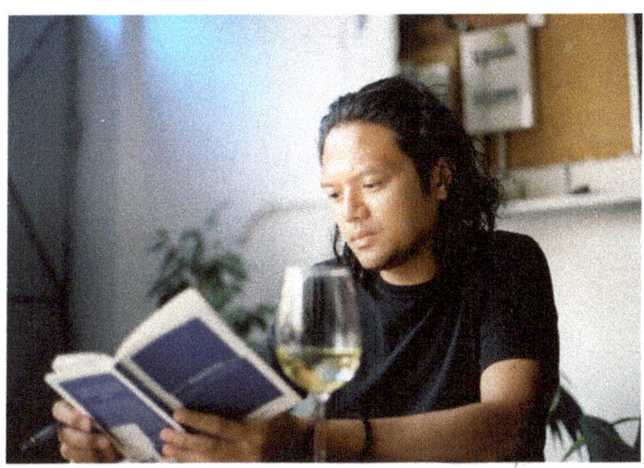

Jeremy Fernando reads, writes, and makes things.

He works in the intersections of literature, philosophy, and art; and his, more than thirty, books include *Reading Blindly, Living with Art, Writing Death, in fidelity, Tómate un paseo por el lado oscuro del camino, resisting art, Writing Skin, A Ghost Never Dies, The feather of Ma'at, un oeil d'or, I wish we were lovers,* and *Jeremy Fernando by Jeremy Fernando.* His writing has also been featured in magazines and journals such as *Arte al Límite, Berfrois, CTheory, Cenobio, Entropy, Full Bleed, Poiesis, Philosophy World Democracy, Queen Mob's Teahouse, Qui Parle, RIC Journal, Testo e Senso, TimeOut,* and *Voice & Verse Poetry Magazine,* amongst others; and has been translated into the Brazilian-Portuguese, French, German, Italian, Japanese, Korean, Spanish, and Serbian. Exploring other media has led him to film, music, performance-readings, and the visual arts; and his work has been exhibited in Seoul, Vienna, Hong Kong, Lisbon, and Singapore. He has been invited to read at the *Akademie der Künste* in Berlin in September 2016; and to deliver a series of performance-readings at the 2018, 2020, and 2022 editions of the *Bienal de la Imagen en Movimiento* in Buenos Aires, the latter at which he also curated a filmic omnibus entitled *reading dreaming malaya.*

He is the general editor of Delere Press; curates the thematic magazine *One Imperative;* is the Jean Baudrillard Fellow at The European Graduate School; co-creator of the private dining experience, People Table Tales; and the writer-in-residence at Appetite, the sensorial laboratory exploring the cross-roads of food, music, and art.

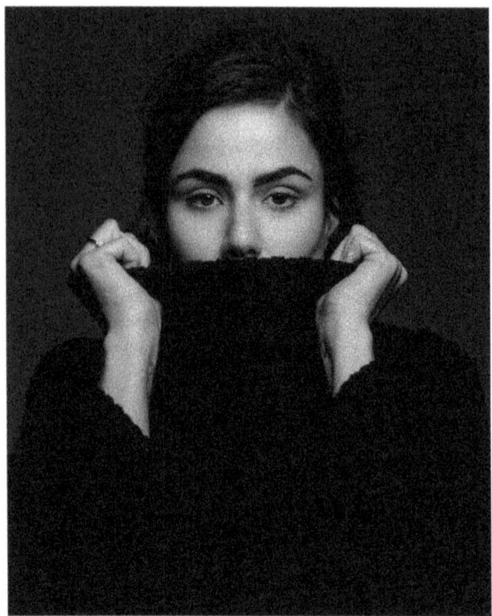

Laima Leyton is a Brazilian artist currently based in London, U.K. Her practice fuses music, performance, education, and readymade.

Throughout her work, sounds are the main tool to weave unique narratives that include elements of audience interaction. Leyton uses questions and actions to connect herself and the audience. *Home* (released in 2019) is Leyton's conceptual album about motherhood and domestic life. It was performed in people's homes until 2022, when Leyton broke the narrative, moved towards a conventional music event, and performed *Home* at The Purcell Room (Southbank Centre). During her performances, Leyton modified domestic objects such as the washing machine to play synth sounds and effects such as reverbs and filters. This act is true to Leyton's practice and brings domestication, migration, spirituality, and motherhood into the spotlight.

Leyton's residency at Gasworks (as InnerSwell) linked local communities to the making and memory of sounds. She is a resident artist at Gasworks. Leyton has received a fellowship from the charity In Place of War and is represented by the Richard Saulton Gallery (London) and as a musician by UTA. For her most recent project, Leyton created a durational performance in response to "Acts Of Resistance: Photography, Feminism and the Art of Protest" at the South London Gallery in May 2024. Leyton is also a mother, a music producer, and part of the Belgian band Soulwax.

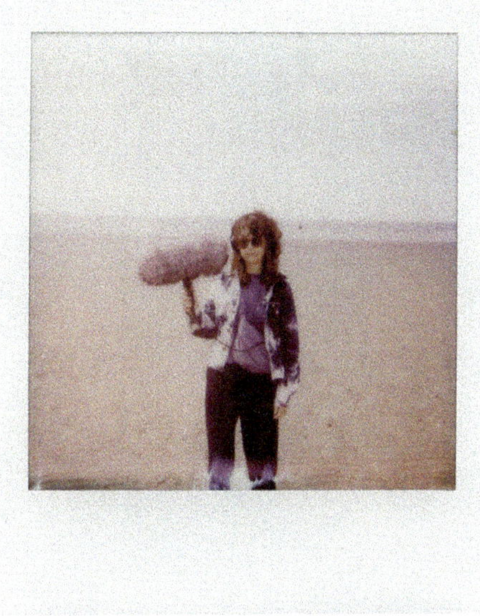

Ecka Mordecai is an artist working across sonic, performative and olfactory disciplines.

Her early studies were in Elizabethan and Renaissance music (Viola de Gamba, Rebec, Recorder) and Classical cello. She later attended art schools in Brighton and London, specialising in sound and performance art. Between 2010 and 2020 she worked primarily in improvisation, developing extended techniques for cello which took inspiration from the British free-improv movement and text scores of the 1960/70s Fluxus art movement. After 2020 her work became more compositional, exploring themes of intimacy and listening. She composed two solo albums for Cafe Oto's in-house labels Takuroku (*Critique + Prosper*, 2020) and Otoroku (*Promise & Illusion*, 2022), a collection of soundscape-inspired perfumes for Aequill (*Sound 01/02/03*, 2022), and composed for Kamila Kuc's experimental short film *I Was There* (2025).

She has a project with Valerio Tricoli (*Mordecoli, Château Mordécoly*, 2022) and is in a trio with Andrew Chalk and Tom James Scott (*Circæa, The Bridge of Dreams*, 2017). She works as a sound technician and educator at University of the Arts, London.

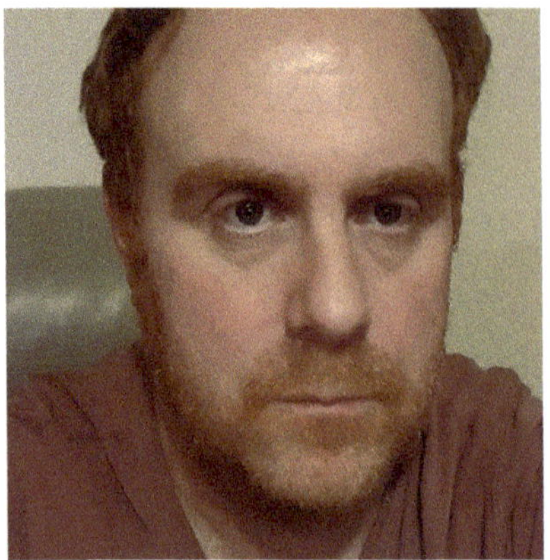

Dara Waldron teaches on the Critical and Contextual program at Limerick School of Art and Design at the Technological University of the Shannon (Midlands/Midwest). He is the author of *Cinema and Evil: Moral Complexities and the "Dangerous" Film* (2013) and *New Nonfiction Film: Art, Poetics and Documentary Theory* (2018). Dara has published extensively in international journals, most notably *Studies in Documentary Film, Millennium Film Journal, Alphaville, Herri, The Moving Image Review* and *Art Journal* and *Found Footage Magazine*. He is a regular contributor to Irish independent media and politics journal *Cassandra Voices*. In recent years Dara has been a visiting professor at Dalarna University (Sweden), Aalto University (Finland) and the University of Colorado, Boulder (US).

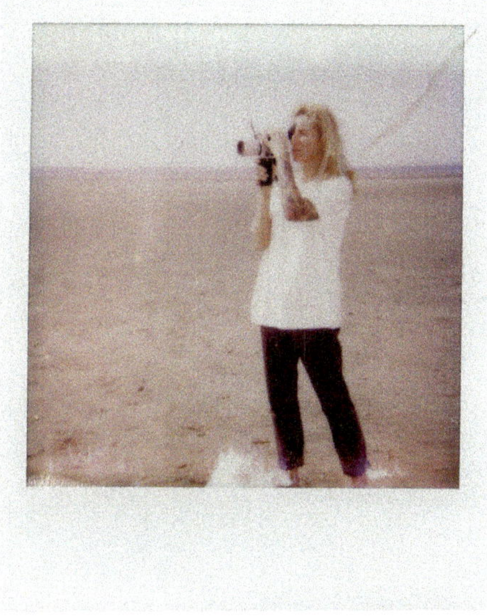

Kamila Kuc is a Polish-born, London/Seattle-based filmmaker, whose hybrid media practice considers complex ways to relate to one another through embodied, care and trust-building practices that foster collaboration and co-creation. She is the Founder and Director of Dark Spring Studio, a London-based production company dedicated to the creation and distribution of artist moving image works that are committed to social change. Her films have screened at many festivals and galleries worldwide: the Edinburgh International Film Festival, National Gallery, Washington, DC, CROSSROADS, Ann Arbor Film Festival, Anthology Film Archives New York; Studio Gallery, Warsaw; Whitechapel Gallery, BFI, ICA, London. Her work has recently been extensively reviewed by a leading documentary film scholar, Dara Waldron in the 10th edition of *Found Footage Magazine* (October 2024).